C000259826

This book is dedicated to my friend Alex
who died giving such love to the world and to all my family,
friends, clients, teachers and the Miracle of loving thought that
creates MIRACLES like you and me that can choose to think
thoughts of PEACE, LOVE & FORGIVENESS.

©2003 Roger King
3 Waterton Close, Walton, Wakefield,
West Yorkshire WF2 6JT U.K.

Email: roger@soultalkstories.com
Visit the website at www.soultalkstories.com

The moral right of the author has been asserted.
Illustrations by John Welding

First Published 2003
Second Print 2004
Third Print 2005
Printed in England by Harris Bros., Featherstone, West Yorkshire

Roger King

"…We'll be hearing a lot more about this book 'Love The Miracle You Are', thank you Roger King."

Kevin Howells, D.J. BBC Leeds Radio

"…I think your book is well written, I'd like to help you get your story into a major newspaper and into the states."

Hilary Robinson, Journalist & Children's Author

"The thoughts and feelings in this book come straight from the heart."

Jane, Youth Worker

"… I read your book this evening and it could have been written about me."

Alex

"…I am reading your book, I didn't realise I had so much to learn about me, I'll sell it in my shop."

Steve, Health Food Manager & Entrepreneur

" …I have read your book and it has opened my eyes to what's possible!"

Julie, Personal Assistant

"This book needs to be read by anybody wanting to think in their own mind & willing to learn to love the MIRACLE they truly are. I loved it."

Pete

Postscript

Roger has received letters, phone calls and e-mails thanking him for this book – He would like to thank all readers for their positive feedback.

CONTENTS

A note to the reader   Page 4

Part I
A Personal Journey

CHAPTER 1
My Evolving Beliefs   Page 7

CHAPTER 2
Starting to Dissolve the Oughts & Should   Page 13

CHAPTER 3
My Story   Page 21

Part II
Recognising & Overcoming the Blocks

CHAPTER 4
Anger & Guilt   Page 35

CHAPTER 5
Criticism & Fear   Page 43

CHAPTER 6
Creating a Positive Inner ParentTo Love Our Inner Child   Page 51

Part III
Trusting the Power Within

CHAPTER 7
Learning to Trust The Power That Made Us & That's Within Us   Page 63

CHAPTER 8
We Can Change the World by Changing Our Selves   Page 71

CHAPTER 9
Empowerment   Page 81

Part IV
Moving On

CHAPTER 10
Giving Thanks for Being Heard by Someone Special   Page 89

CHAPTER 11
Soul Talk Creates Conscious Freedom   Page 101

CHAPTER 12
What is the Purpose of it All?   Page 109

RECOMMENDED READING   Page119

A Note To You The Reader

If you are inspired by the ideas in this book, and ready, please consider choosing to write your own healing story about: "LOVE THE MIRACLE YOU ARE".

Visit www.soultalkstories.com on the Internet and click on "stories".

Part I
A Personal Journey

CHAPTER 1
My Evolving Beliefs

"When I love myself enough I learned to stop what I am doing, if even for a moment, and comfort the part of me that is scared."
Kim and Alison McMillen

This book is about positive change and growth and about re-parenting ourselves so we can love who we are from a place of respect and reconnect to the miracle we were when conceived and born. One of the biggest freedoms for me was to realise nobody can think in my mind except me! I control my mind, not my parents, teachers, friends, politicians or any religious faith leaders. Yet we learned as children about life and about ourselves from the limiting beliefs and reactions of the adults around us. Many of us come from families where our parents (or their substitutes) did not love themselves. Consequently it would be hard, if not impossible, for each of us to love ourselves from a place of deep respect.

"If I don't love me how can I really love God or my neighbour?"

My life is very simple, yet at times not easy; it is learning to love the miracle of me, not selfishly, then helping others to love themselves, if they are willing. I have also learnt that if I really want to change and grow; I need to learn about how my mind works then use it with a higher loving intention. If you want to change your life, ask and challenge yourself with this question:

"Do I really want to change and grow?"

"Am I willing to do what it takes even when the going can get tough?"

The answer is deep inside you; I believe that there is a power and an actualising tendency in all of us, to become all that we can be. Just watch a baby learning to walk; they never give up no matter how many falls they experience. Each of us has within us vast resources for self-understanding, for altering our self-image, our beliefs and attitudes that help us mentally, emotionally, physically and spiritually in our learning to grow. The desire toward "constructive fulfillment" is present in us all. I believe it is our birthright to find the miracle of love, creativity, healing, joy, and learn our unique spiritual lessons that returns us to the power that created us.

Once when I was collapsing from mental and emotional overload I came across a book called "Carl Rogers on Personal Power". I was about to give a lecture on starting a small business. I had gone to the library at Lancaster university crying out inside for help, when (by divine guidance) this book just stared out at me from all the thousands of books. I bought the book immediately and on the train home I read the book, as though my life had meaning, even when I felt I had no personal power. This one book helped me to start searching for a new way to build self-worth and live my life with trust and love of life.

I believe that when my life gets desperate and I honestly face myself (like the desert experience of those seeking their relationship with God) a higher power guides and protects me. My deep intention is signalled to the power within my higher self and all that I need to grow and change is brought to me. Yet life does not have to get desperate. The more we go within and ask, "What is it you want me to learn?" The answers will come; patience will need to be learnt. So often we are impatient in learning the steps to loving who we truly are. "This is resistance to learning", suggests Louise Hay.

I believe, when we really want to grow, and we go within, often with considerable resistance at first, we connect to this power and that gradually directs us to our highest good. For me this continued when my first marriage was coming close to ending, I experienced physical exhaustion from work that did not use my talents. I felt being a father and a man was my biggest problem. I saw myself as a "problem", not as a human being. I was totally out of contact with my feelings and even though I had studied psychology, I knew only how to cope with masks and facades I could not listen to myself with any acceptance, only critically and blame my past.

I believe that if we really want to change, we first have to learn to accept ourselves just as we are. Learning to listen carefully to you is a key to truthful and positive growth. It seems a paradox that when I accept myself or I am listened to with deeper understanding as I am, I begin to change positively. I have learned from all my clients that we cannot move away from what we are until we accept who we are now and without saying we are bad or wrong. YOU AND I HAVE DONE THE BEST YOU AND I KNOW HOW, TO GET WHERE WE ARE NOW. Congratulate yourself that you are reading this book, you are probably seeking change yet don't know how! This is not to patronise you, change without guilt is what I want to achieve for myself.

> *"Guilt only attracts punishment and punishment seeks pain."*
>
> (Louise Hay)

As I accept who I am and I internalise a new belief, "Whatever we give out we get back multiplied", or as the Bible says, "Do unto others as you want done unto you," I would add without guilt, then I believe we begin to take back our personal power. We come to trust our intuitive soul, our body, our minds, our higher self and we move from being a victim of victims, to seeing we are personally responsible for our lives. Then we cease blaming anybody including ourselves. This is when change begins to be experienced in positive ways and we begin waking up looking forward to the day and spending quality time with ourselves and others. There are "25,000 hours of old tapes stored in our subconscious mind," says John Bradshaw, many of these tapes don't support us now.

Remember that beliefs are patterns of thoughts and feelings (ideas) we have taken in from childhood. The more negative our upbringing the more hardened our patterns are by the age of 5-7 years of age. We accept these as true for ourselves like "stupid, spoilt, fat, too thin, ugly, everybody is going to reject me, I am not good enough, I am not worthy or I don't deserve, I can't trust anybody including me." So then as we grow, these beliefs (rigid negative thinking, feeling patterns) underpin a very poor self-talk inside our heads, no matter how we disguise ourselves. The more negative our programming the more susceptible we are to feeling we will be found out as "not good enough." This can lead to intricate or complex coping mechanisms that may include negative obsessions or addictions.

So often a client says "I am probably one of your worst clients. I don't know what you will think of me." The more I can create a climate of me being real and value the person I am relating to and truly empathise with them, reflecting what is just beneath the level of awareness, this then becomes an exciting journey of self-discovery to them learning to love who they are without manipulation. I never buy into them saying, "I am unlovable".

The more I go through life I see people's beliefs can either support them positively or more often negatively. Yet dismantling or dissolving negative beliefs is to be handled in a climate of respect, love and transparent honesty where trust has to be built.

I believe, the more I am willing to be myself and accept the other person, with their complexity; the more a paradox comes into being. Constructive change comes about in the client and ironically in those people they are in relationship to. Whatever is going on inside us we attract to us in outer experience. If I hate myself I will most probably attract to me other people who hate themselves. This can have negative consequences in whom I choose to have relationships with, the work I do, my health and all areas of my life. Just look at your experiences in life now, if they are negative be willing to see how that is a reflection of how you think and feel about yourself. Please don't beat yourself up, just be willing to learn how to love you. Rome was not built in one day!

"We are each responsible for our experiences".

When I first heard that from a Buddhist teacher I wanted to kick him and myself!

TAKING BACK RESPONSIBILITY FOR OUR DECISIONS IN LIFE IS A CRUCIAL STEP TO LOVING YOURSELF

The hard part at first is holding the mirror to you, for example taking responsibility for the decision we made to enter an intimate relationship that we now find unloving and possibly abusive. Taking responsibility is being willing to grow and change you, rather than the partner. I always wanted my first wife to change then life would be OK. If the partner will not change then we may have to love ourselves out of that relationship. Responsibility is taking back the power we have so often given away by blaming others and ourselves. The sooner we drop blame, I believe, all good can come into our life. We need to release the past and forgive everyone including ourselves.

This may take time, with a few stages on the way. I talk about this at length later in the book. I was brought up not to trust people, so I attracted to me people and situations that I could not trust and I certainly could not forgive. However as I start to go within and connect to this loving, creative power that you may call the power within, or universal source, I call God or infinite source (just watch your reaction to that concept), mistrust gradually dissolves.

My personal experience of God means love and "will" means "thought". So for me the discovery that God's will is "loving thoughts," not a condemning source, which I learnt at home and in church as a reluctant choirboy, is a revelation. Then the love within us that made us a miracle of life is the source for all good. The more we learn to tap this source and become 'at one' or 'in tune' with loving thoughts the more our life unfolds to the highest level for all involved, including healing our planet. So whatever you believe about yourself will come true for you! Learn the steps to building loving thoughts in your mind.

Think how many thoughts you have in one day, many thousands, and ask yourself right now, "What am I attracting to me now?" How many of those thoughts are thinking what you don't want in your life, rather than what you do want? This one realisation can change your life. What you are thinking right now is creating your future, so ask yourself, "Is what I am thinking right now going to create a great future?" If the answer is "no," then you are free to choose positive thoughts to change your negative thoughts right now. My sister recently broke her leg in three places. Not denying the pain she made a vow to learn from every challenge she met, and being determined she would heal and grow from the experience physically, mentally and spiritually, she is doing exactly that. At times she has suffered setbacks, waking up feeling sorry for herself, then becoming aware of her thoughts she started thinking thoughts that supported her healing. Loving yourself means treating yourself as deserving the best from yourself and life.

After years of my own therapy and working to help others I have found we have far more in common than differences. Yes we are each unique, yet when we get past the masks and we become closer to another person we realise the following powerful thought from Louise Hay. *"Everyone is dealing with the damaging patterns of resentment, criticism, guilt and self-hatred."*

Clients often describe themselves as a bad person yet this is a thought that "they are hating" and I believe the thought that is so powerful here is: *"These are only thoughts, and thoughts can be changed."* Each of us has the power to change what we are choosing to think in our minds. I cannot think in your mind; you control what you are thinking right now in your mind! State the thought in your mind now: *"I love and accept myself exactly as I am and it is safe to change"*. If you persistently repeat this thought, especially into a mirror, then positive change and growth begins, despite your resistance. Little by little you will believe you deserve love. I go into detail through the book. These power points have helped me from Louise Hay's book *"You can Heal Your Life."*

1. *"We are each responsible for our experiences."*
2. *"Every thought we think is creating our future."*
3. *"Everyone is dealing with damaging patterns of resentment, criticism, guilt and self-hatred."*
4. *"These are only thoughts and thoughts can be changed."*
5. *"We need to release the past and forgive everyone."*
6. *"Self-approval and self-acceptance in the 'now' are the keys to positive change."*
7. *"The point of power is always in the present moment."*

I would add this my own power thought:

"By choosing to think "loving thoughts" we allow and receive all good, and our lives unfold to their highest level."
(You may find it helpful to keep a personal journal as you complete some of the exercises.)

LOVE CANNOT CO-EXIST WITH FEAR
Remember, the thoughts we have create our world and our experiences. The more we communicate with the inner power, for our guidance, then we will radiate love and the more our life will unfold with meaning and purpose. When I talk of learning to love you, I am asking you to come from a place of deep respect within you. This is not ego, not wanting power over, that is fear.

As you learn to follow simple rules like "WHAT WE GIVE OUT, WE GET BACK", just catch what you are thinking right now, is it positive or negative? Do you want this thought to be creating your future experience?

EXERCISE
Write out your thoughts and reactions to the above power points. Read them out loud to yourself and then share them with partner or friends.

CHAPTER 2
Starting to Dissolve the Should & Ought & I Can't

"The greatest danger for most of us is not that our aim is too high and we miss it, but that it is too low and we reach it."
Michelangelo

I remember sitting as a child being told by a visiting uncle, "I ought to be 'a good boy' for my parents because you might upset them." I can remember being told at five on my first day at school that "I should not cry like a baby." My punishment was being put in a corner with my face against the wall and thinking "all I want is my mum." I learned very early from my father that a boy should not cry and if I did cry, the statement came back, "If you keep on crying, I will really give you something to cry about!" Whenever I hear that statement in a street or café by parents to children who are yelling, my blood runs high. I am sure you, the reader, can remember some of the 'should' statements that were made to you, and the associated words, "no you can't do that, it's too dangerous."

The 'I can't' feeling came painfully to me recently, when I visited an art gallery. I asked myself why is it so painful for me to look at art? Then I was transported back to my first proper art lesson, being a scruffy 6 year-old sitting at a square desk that had ink stains and a small grey piece of rough paper upon which I was doodling. I loved drawing just how I felt; I was not drawing the apple on the desk at the front of class. When the teacher came up from behind, I can remember the musty smell she had of perfume and paint. She said "King, you are no good at drawing;

you have no talent at all, look at how good the others are; you are just wasting my time." My inner child collapsed in shame, I went red and shivered with guilt and felt so bad. This feeling of "I can't" just loomed up and I vowed to never let anybody see any drawing or painting I did again." What a deep negative affirmation.

I can remember being told "I should go to church every Sunday" by my parents and dutifully did, yet watched my parents hardly ever go. Our brain is geared for honesty and truth, yet often as children, we receive a mixed message that confuses our child-brain that wants to be loyal and be good, yet feels "I am a bad boy." Later, as we grow, this becomes an internalised negative affirmation of never feeling good enough!

When I listen to clients talk about how they 'should be,' I get a sense of the small inner child telling me how mother, father, teacher, minister, even God, wanted them to be. If you take any child and tell it "no" all the time and hit or smack it, the life energy and thinking patterns become warped for survival instead of how wonderful life can be. Here is an unfolding story of one young man.

A TRUE STORY THAT IS CONTINUING!

A man was found wondering on a roadside, thinking thoughts of giving up his life. A lovely couple that knew him stopped their car and just listened to him speak of the crisis he was in. The couple themselves had recently been through a personal crisis, so they knew to help him by listening and not judging. Then, on his choice he came to see me. His story was of a boy who had been hit physically and emotionally by a father who hated him and his mother.

He often tried to protect his mother, yet failed by taking a beating himself. He had deep negative mental and emotional patterns of being second best to his brother, who he felt got everything. At school he was consistently bullied and, if that was not enough, he always felt blamed for anything that went wrong both at home and at school. All of this emotional baggage, and much more, went into a runaway relationship with a teenage woman of 13 when he was 16.

Many years later all his negative beliefs about himself came to the surface when his wife walked out and left him looking after their three children, two of which were under 6 years old. As he poured out his violent childhood and teenage years, I sensed he was desperate to find out that there must be more to life than his experience of life so far. He wanted to be a good husband and father, yet had little knowledge how to do this or any good role model to learn from.

After one session this emotionally battered man with an emotional age of anywhere between 6-30 years was willing to do one thing. He was willing to learn how to value his life rather than keep heaping negative messages of blame and self-hatred upon himself.

What I experienced deep inside me as I listened was a soul with so many reasons to blame and hate the world, yet he was willing to trust me enough and give himself a real chance to love the "True Miracle" deep inside. He took his power back (responsibility) and was open to learning new thoughts that could change his life for the better, despite what everyone else thought of him! He went home and started reading the first edition of this book and listened to an audio CD of the book as well as lots of other self-help tapes.

He made a decision to love himself from a place of deep self respect and then practice positive affirmations as much as he could. Each time he hit fear, guilt, shame and all the old messages stored in his subconscious mind, he was willing to go to the mirror and say, "I love and approve of myself" and many more affirmations. This inner discipline of dissolving the 'should not' and 'I can't' with positive tapes and occasional supportive phone calls to friends and myself, gave him that spark to grow his inner awareness.

As he grew he left an extreme right wing political party and chose to visit his mum who he had not seen for 7 years. The meeting was a good one! He knows it is a continuing journey of healing by learning to love his life, yet he is willing. Are you willing to let go your past and love YOU?

When we are told we are "stupid" or "should not have been born" and many other messages, the subconscious mind believes it and relays this to the conscious mind, so much so we create experiences that confirm those negative taped messages. We just begin to hate and this thought pattern hurts us physically, mentally and, if we still have any spiritual faith, we can be left with a perception of a God that is punishing and hates us.

I have just read this section out loud to the person who is in this story. He said he wanted it included in this revised book to encourage you, the reader, and added this personal note:

There is much more I could say, yet what I will say is:
"There are so many good reasons to love yourself rather than not!"

SEEING HOW WE THINK

The injunctions, the way we think inside our heads can leak our personal power. In the early sessions of counselling, I often see the person become furious at his or her own sense of giving away their power. One particular lady came and poured out her story of childhood abuse, her mother died when she was three, she was pushed from one home to another. In her own thinking (through her taking in what was told to her) she was stupid and only good for one thing. By five she was raped, from then on her self-esteem went through the floor. When her mother died she was sent to her older sister's home, the uncle then abused her emotionally and physically. She tried going back to her father but he was drunk, always she felt completely alone.

Then as she grew sex became a way of getting some of her needs met, yet at a terrible price. She eventually got married to a man she hated and her life became a fight to bring up three children without hurting them. She became a Christian and at first this helped her, then this got so entangled with subtle abuse from her church. By the time she entered counselling she just cried and sobbed. What I saw through all her pain and hurt was an intelligent, strong-willed woman. I challenged her with this perception and asked; are you willing to learn and work? She was, and her quick intelligent mind started reading everything I suggested. She would come and tell me what she was learning, her whole awareness leapt, she said in one session. "WHY AREN'T WE TAUGHT HOW TO USE OUR MINDS IN WAYS THAT TRULY SUPPORT US?" Her real change came when she 'got it'. She would not allow memories from the past, or anybody else to invade her determination to improve the way she used her mind; she could choose what she was going to think in her mind. She was learning to love the person she was, discovering a person that had the capacity to love, learn, and parent her children in more loving ways.

This was not egotistical love, from fear; it was the dawn of new thinking. She realised she deserved the best from herself and life, accepting she wasn't perfect. What came out of her mouth was no longer swear words, her words conveyed self-approval and a deep respect for whom she was. The last time I saw her, she put money on my desk to buy some books she thought I would find exciting and then told me her husband had signed over the business to her. She had sold £68,000 of the product in three months. I asked her "How?" She replied, "By listening carefully to the women who came to buy and changing the product accordingly." This lady is now a successful businessperson, with a deep faith in a loving God and herself. Again she has learnt to love herself past old limiting beliefs and choosing beliefs that support her life and consequently she is prospering in health, time, positive relationships and money. This person gives a lot of healing out to others and chooses carefully whom she relates to. Before, she always attracted relationships that put her down and this replayed the past when she was bullied at school, at home and in her church relationships.

I cannot state enough, how courageous a person is to make a decision from being a victim to learning they are worth loving and gradually cease blaming themselves.

THE "I CANT'S" INSIDE YOUR HEAD

One obstacle for many people is the "I can't". For example, "I can't study. I am uneducated". This often comes from being criticised at school and reinforced later at work or no work. Yet once the person has seen clearly what they are doing to themselves, i.e. just carrying on criticising, a thought they choose to think about themselves and what they are choosing to say in their mind, it's as though a light goes on inside them and they start reading, attending lectures on subjects that they feel are relevant to their growth and building new supportive relationships. Some call it "revelation from God", for me, it may be far less dramatic, just an honest intelligent inner conversation with yourself that the universal power recognises and starts giving you real opportunities to improve your life.

Once you make a deep decision, from what many call your higher self, to change and let go of the past, live in the present, then positively think and speak what you want in the future, your life will change in ways you cannot imagine.

Then we can give thanks and mean it, remember that more good will come to you as you give thanks for everything in your life. If you have been emotionally, physically, sexually and/or spiritually abused, or been in a difficult relationship, remember the point of power is in the present moment. There is so much help, reach out to find good counsellors and/or read books that are suggested in the back of this book. Repeat this affirmation as often as you can remember or make your own.

" I love and approve of myself and I attract to me now, people and resources that help me think and see clearly in my mind. I respect me. I let go of all need to blame others and myself. And so it is."

If you can't believe this affirmation just start with...

'I am willing to learn to love me.'

Start where you can in developing your affirmation, the universe will bring the how.

CO-DEPENDENCY

Often people with strict faiths with self-punishing beliefs take the longest to believe they are worth loving and trustworthy, due to subtle or not so subtle internalised messages from childhood. Parental figures and sometimes clergy often portray the fear of an unloving, punishing, all-seeing God day after day. This can create such divided loyalties, especially in a person who finds it difficult to think in their own mind. For example the sin of safe enjoyable sex in religious families and institutions has become like a secret weapon to keep people oppressed and stay in low self-worth. This has increased abuse of all kinds, which is gradually changing when we learn what a valuable magnificent miracle we truly are. For me to help create a climate where somebody feels truly trustworthy, where they have vast inner resources for self-understanding, for altering their self-concept and direct their own thinking and behaviour is so freeing. Often a client will describe feeling disloyal, pulled in so many directions as they start the journey of choosing to think for themselves, trusting their own deep wisdom, realising we can each have our own relationship with God is not easy.

My 14 year-old daughter returned from a workshop on religion last night where she felt she could not say her own opinion. Unusually for her she felt unsafe to speak out, she shared the dynamics from her point of view. And I quote *"Last week we were told we would be respected if we disagreed with anything that is said in the talk. This week we were 'talked at' and I felt there was no room for being heard. If I did say anything I would not be heard, I chose not to lay myself open to being criticised"*. This was a painful yet learning experience, as tears came she spoke powerfully to us about how she admires her strength in saying what she believes. I know my daughter does not want to be a victim to this situation and blame herself or others; she is growing from this unfolding experience. Many of us have been in situations where we feel unsafe to express our own thoughts on a subject, protecting our deep feelings inside. Creating a safe inner environment for ourselves is a vital stage in growth and is a positive change. My daughter is presently starting her first small book; I admire her courage and wisdom.

WE DO HAVE A CHOICE!

I believe once we move from being a victim of victims, there is a power inside each one of us that is waiting to give us such abundant good, once we stop blaming and criticising and we start being open to new ideas that we can make our own, in our own unique way. Some people say to me *"Oh you're reading Louise Hay, she talks about loving yourself!"* Without justifying myself I reply *"I am willing to learn from people who are further along the path of life in learning to love themselves from a place of respect. If I can learn to grow in a healthier loving and truly giving way I then may have something useful to say and give to this planet"*. I want this book to be me as I learn about the process of loving the miracle within me; positive role models who reflect what I deeply trust is truthful, I am willing to learn from. So please bear with me on this inner and outer journey. I end this chapter with the most powerful thought that helped me begin a new step in my awareness.

"I love and approve of myself exactly as I am."

Louise Hay

"As I say yes to loving thoughts, the more loving thoughts say yes to me."

My Inner Child

In a nutshell, for me the higher self is teaching us to re-love ourselves with a deep integrity of positive thought that evolves into a personal relationship with God. Many of us were brought up to be co-dependent on other's negative beliefs about ourselves. Then we want to blame and expect others to change, without us doing anything, or we want to be told what to think and then we can stay a victim, by blaming others when our lives go wrong. Well that's not how it is. The more we learn to create intelligent and practical ways of communicating within, by taking responsibility for everything we think, say and do, we then mean business to change and grow, without guilt. The more we see the negative 'payoffs' and we release those intelligently with love and forgiveness, the universe takes notice and we grow towards our highest good. The miracle of life breathes a whole new language and story! And so it is.

EXERCISE

Write 'I ought'; at the top of a piece of paper, then finish the sentence with your first thought. Then write in between, 'Who told you that?' or 'Where did you learn this?' Then ask yourself, "WHAT DO I GET FROM STAYING WITH THIS OUGHT?" The answer will often be a negative payoff, which becomes a self-destructive behaviour and creates a negative experience that produces a victim mentality.

Examples

1. *"I ought to go to church every Sunday."* (My parents told me I would be seen as bad and sinful if I didn't.) Negative payoff is I don't have to think much, and I feel I have done penance!

2. *"I ought to send Christmas cards to everyone."* (My mum and dad sent cards every year and got in such a panic that they might forget someone.) The payoff is I want others to send me one and like me.

3. *"I ought to please my husband when he wants sex and I don't."* (That's what my mum told me. I have learnt to lie there and let him have his way.) The payoff He'll get angry if I don't and I will cop it or the kids will, it keeps the peace!

4. *"I ought to be much more clever and extrovert."* (The teachers and my dad told me I wasn't clever and people at work tell me I am boring to be around.) Well it makes life easier I can watch TV and chill out and be lazy, nobody expects too much from me.

5. *"I ought to have better legs and lose weight."* (Well just look at the fashion magazines and my boy friends have confirmed that I am too fat!) The payoff is I can eat and drink what I like by appearing not to care.

6. *"I ought not to have been born!"* (My mum when she was cross with me shouted this at me and made me look at her when she said it. Now when anything goes wrong, I find myself saying the same.) Well the payoff is I can always blame me more than anybody else can blame me. I suppose I am my worst critic. I reject me before others do. That sounds pretty neurotic! I suppose I am frightened of getting really intimate. I hate anybody telling me off. I want approval all the time.

CHAPTER 3
My Story

You cannot be taught how to love yourself when your parents never learnt how to love themselves. Yet listening to parents with the intention of forgiveness in your heart about their childhood can release you all, from continued hate, fear, criticism and guilt. Then forgiveness opens the door to the heart. Forgiveness begins with the one who recognizes the offence. When you get the offence out of your own heart, you have forgiven. The reconciliation, which you do within yourself, will have healing effects on all that have hurt you and for who you have hurt.

PART OF MY STORY
During the early stages of counselling I ask clients about their childhood. Whatever problems and patterns of thinking and behaving they have now, have often originated in early parenting. As a child from two to ten years of age, I would sing in bed before going to sleep with a blue blanket over my face, like lots of young children I would go into another reality. One favourite song was *"Grand Old Duke Of York, he had 10,000 men, he'd march them up to the top of the hill and he'd march them down again."*

As I look back on my nightly singing, it was a reaction to a deep need to comfort my scared child that hated hearing my parents quarrel and the paper thin walls that heard what I interpreted as my mother crying and my father needing sex. Her father had sexually abused my mother; so one huge ghost would rear its ugly head for me nearly every night. My mother inappropriately repeatedly told me, of her "rotten father" and how men only wanted sex! And added, "never be like your father," this was a tape that re-played for years and haunted me. If my mother ever wanted to scold me, all she had to say was *"you're just like your father"* and I would collapse inside. *"Everything makes sense when you know the complete and true history."*

So this child interpreted being a male was "bad". This message was not a healthy internal belief for a male child, teenager and young man. From my early memories I can remember wanting to be different in gender and in every other area of my life.

When I went to school I had low self-esteem, this I believe attracted being bullied by boys and schoolteachers, the latter emotionally and intellectually. So my ability to learn at school was spent surviving. Gradually, I hated school. I remember one of my headmasters at secondary school saying, "King 2," (my other nick name was "Mooney", I hated it) "you are a complete failure and I doubt if you'll make anything of yourself." Not a healthy message to give a young mind. I vowed to myself I would leave school as soon as I was fifteen, just to get away and I did. This shows how powerful our vowed thoughts can be!

Just before I left school I had a taste of fear and anger. I was surrounded by a huge mob taunting me. I shouted, "I will take one of you on" and out stepped my nightmare bully. Suddenly I lost my fear and like "the incredible hulk" I nearly killed this boy. It took three masters to pull me off. The anger inside me erupted like an uncontrollable volcano. I then reverted back to fear of myself; my fear was that I could kill someone if I allowed myself to feel anger. In therapy, years later I located what John Bradshaw calls "the uncovery process". This was attached to the anger I felt towards my father, from early childhood. Underneath the anger was grief. I spent years wanting to cry, yet my subconscious mind repeated the one big should that came down from my father that many boys and men have internalised: "Never show your feelings or cry, you cannot trust anybody if you show your emotions". I didn't realise Lao-tzu's saying would come true for me,

"To give no trust is to get no trust."

My sisters expressed their fear of what was going on between our parents by being angry at each other, while I reverted to being fearful of life always expecting the worst to happen. This pattern of thinking attracted lots of relationships that were frightening. I thought for years that nobody else had fearful thoughts and feelings like mine. I learnt to live inside my head and create a reality of fear.

These messages and many more came from a father who was clearly never taught how to love himself. On listening to my father in later years about his early childhood, I received clear pictures, of a young boy parenting himself. His mother was physically and emotionally absent, often drinking to escape her emotional pain. My father had a tough childhood, yet the saving grace for my father was his father, who believed in him and his brother. The pain in my father and mother surfaced in deep mistrust that so often undermined their love for each other. Both had so little self-awareness of how to parent three children and how to listen and understand each other. They had so little idea of how to play or spend quality time with us; all this was a reaction to their parenting.

One important drive in both parents was to give us a "better upbringing than theirs." I realise my parents did the best with what they knew. Now with time, I thank them both for what they gave me, even the tough times. I never knew the ancient mystical Jewish saying taken from the Kabbalah: " *The falls of our life provide us with the energy to propel ourselves to a higher level*".

I went through a long time of blaming my parents; this kept me stuck in the past and was one of the hardest times in my life. As I have learnt to understand these two wounded people, I learnt how to forgive and love them. This has taken time, in therapy where I released lots of anger safely. Letting go of my anger in a safe place was a vital element in learning to forgive and realising I had the power within me, to change how I reacted and thought about my whole family. This was so "freeing". I see clearly now, that I had such a confirmed belief that I was a waste of space and only deserved the worst. "They" out there were only being a mirror of my beliefs.

'Changing the externals does not change your internal world and what that keeps attracting to you.'

IMPORTANT PEOPLE AT CRITICAL TIMES

The importance of new people in my life came when I left school at fifteen and I met Alex Dickson, who ran a project called "Community Volunteers". He interviewed me and gave me my first responsible job in caring for ex-prisoners in Leeds, Yorkshire. This job tested and again mirrored my fear and anger. I was surrounded by people who had killed, robbed, abused and of course been abused themselves! I stayed for fourteen months. I survived some horrific threats to my life (divine protection?). I had no real awareness that I was attracting to me, people like me inside. I left the project exhausted and returned home to the growing nightmare of my parent's quarrels. My sisters escaped and coped by one getting married and going abroad, while my middle sister got married by getting pregnant. Each of us was doing the best we knew how to survive our subconscious "programming". Later each of us became divorced from our first partners. When you don't love yourself from a place of deep respect the choices we make are often made by rebelling against parents and the system, low self esteem needs so much love even if its just sex! Yet we need so much more.

Not learning or willing to face myself internally, that was too painful, I decided to get some education and the universe brought Gary, the first person who saw something in me that I was totally blind to. That was, I had the ability to study and pass exams, a fear that went deep into my feelings of failure at school.

Over three years, I got any job to support myself, working in a vegetable shop, cleaning, anything to get money. I eventually got into Bradford University to study Psychology, History and Sociology. Then just as I was looking towards freedom, my mother and father asked me to sort out their divorce! This pain of feeling like their parent to their child was too much. I wanted to scream. We sorted their separation and I left to go and be free to learn, so I thought.

ATTRACTING ABUSE WITHOUT AWARENESS

On the first day at college a cynical lecturer told me. *"Don't think you have come here to think for yourself. If you want to succeed, follow and regurgitate what we tell you, then you will do well"*.

This emotional and intellectual abuse was the start of attracting to me, an abuser. He was a senior lecturer at the college who took a great interest in me, groomed me, he made me feel important and asked me to drive his car down to Germany and Austria on a summer school. I was so eager to be thought intelligent enough to be worthy of such a treat. On the second night he got me drunk and tried to rape me. I was so frightened I could not move. The trauma was horrendous. The way I coped with the hurt was feeling I must be gay, what a bizarre rationalisation and reaction. I then went all out to prove I was a man. I attracted to me women who were a reflection of me. I could not trust me, my inner wisdom was unreliable, and I began to hate. I got through university rebelling, joining left wing political parties and had a totally fabricated masked existence. I realise now, how I could have groomed myself to become a so-called 'terrorist!' The damage was done-I felt trapped, I thought I deserved to be treated badly and so I began to do the same.

MASKING THE MASK

I came out of college more frightened and angry and fearful than I went in. My first job was to become part of the establishment. I went for a job in Harley Street, London as a Field Officer for MIND, a mental health charity. Again, I was trying desperately to be accepted by others and totally unwilling to stop and go within to really learn and grow. I met my first wife giving a talk on 'Sanity, Madness and the Family.' My loneliness made me desperate for someone to love me; I hated me, so the only relief was to find somebody who could love what I could not love. I lacked any personal power or responsibility.

So I fell into my first marriage with little self-awareness of what I thought, what I truly wanted from a relationship and what I was prepared to give to a relationship. I could not show or share my feelings I was so full of old negative programming that I must be strong, go out to work and provide the money.

One mental and emotional pattern I carried into my first relationship was, "I must prove myself to be a man." This was an old tape running that did not help me feel good about me. I did try to grow by going to men's groups, I did bodywork therapy and lots of talking in co-counselling yet I was still no closer to learning how to value me and those close to me, including my first wife. It took another twelve years of struggle before we decided to part. I became a social worker working on a rough housing estate in Bristol, trying to help others was a way of denial, yet it was the best I could do with the limited knowledge that I had.

Then I started a small factory for young failures at school that could not get jobs. This exhausted me and distracted me from facing me. I met so-called important people, gave talks and was invited into politics, yet I was falling apart inside. We went as a family to New Zealand to live in a Quaker community to try and solve our marriage. I still didn't get it, that wherever you go, you cannot run away from yourself, your problems go with you. We returned to the UK and then I had an affair, again not facing the truth.

REINFORCING OLD MESSAGES

At this point I felt my mother was right I was just like my father, a "womaniser." My wife and I did the best we knew how with what information we had, we went to counselling and this helped us separate. However the strain was tortuous for us all including our 12 year-old beautiful daughter. I did not take clear responsibility for myself and that I regret.

When we separated I went further into denial rushing into becoming a trainer in industry. Every thing I created was pressure, and in other words I was still scared of facing my life. The more pressure I create in my life now, I ask myself, "What am I scared of learning about myself? What am I not willing to see?" So I left the marriage with guilt, fear and self-hatred. What I attracted to me was a series of disastrous relationships that reflected the same qualities. Every person I had a relationship with had been sexually abused and blamed life, just like me.

A SMALL CHANGE PRODUCED A MASSIVE SHIFT

Then a very small event happened, it was on New Years Eve, I was at a dance, and I sat on the floor while everybody sang AULD LANG SYNE. I just cried out, *"If there is anybody listening all I want is to be with my friends and have no more intimate relationships"*. I admitted to myself that I really wanted to change and I could not carry on as I was going. I wanted to know who I was and stop creating chaos in life. For the first time I became a little more honest with me. Two hours later I met my second wife. We were immediately attracted to each other. Linda was a vision of a person I had dreamed of two years earlier, while fully awake, working out in a gym. I was Linda's vision of what she had dreamt that day.

There is no symbolism here, just a wonderful confirmation: That whatever you put out you get back. I believe my intention changed that evening, some force, energy, God, universal power helped me face me and saw I was willing to grow and not keep on blaming, criticising and being destructively angry. For me a new inner power had led me to my vision. With hindsight you can explain anything, yet all deep personal change comes when you admit to yourself some truth about your own real needs and to start meeting those needs more honestly and gently. I wanted to be loved; I wanted to be re-loved as a baby right the way up to my present age. The universe brought the right soul to do that with and we gave enormous permission to ourselves to just be, even through the storms.

FACING AND LEARNING FROM THE EARLY STORMS

The first two years of our relationship were stormy with both of us working through enormous old tapes of negative programming. We spent a lot of time in therapy and counselling, before we contemplated marriage. I wish that people who want to marry could spend time with creative loving counsellors, helping each person to love who they are and then see if they wish to commit their lives to another person.

Nearly every weekend was spent in some group or growth scene. Some were helpful; others felt more like a clique. I had trained as a personal counsellor years back so I had some reference points to what was guru orientated, that made people more dependant, rather than healthily freeing the individual to learn how to love who they were and think in their own minds.

Often I would test Linda's love for me with a part of me I hated about me, so she could reject me. I couldn't love me so how could she love me? If she didn't reject me I would reject her. Somehow she never bought into me being 'bad', she would listen to my story and say, "well that was tough and that's not you, the person I love." At first I couldn't believe her and then I realised she wanted to have children with me, it was crunch time I had to make a commitment to a person who loved me and certainly loved herself or to get out of the relationship. I made an honest choice to risk loving and being loved; I thank the presence inside me that gave me that wisdom.

My ability to face me, helped me face my daughter from my first marriage, I felt I had let her down badly. She came on a workshop with me called ISA, Institute for Self-Actualisation. This helped us communicate more honestly. We now have a far more honest relationship where she can trust me to be there for her when she needs and wants me. Just recently her newborn son had meningitis and in his wonderful recovery (with thousands of people praying), I felt we grew closer. It takes a lot to make your child lose their love for you, but when that happens, it will take real honest love, by listening, and time spent with each other to rebuild those times of neglect and hurt. Out of this terrible pain and near tragedy with my grandson nearly dying has come good for us all, including my ex-wife and myself. One lesson I learnt "the more I beat myself up with guilt the less able I was to be genuine with my daughter and my ex-wife. The more I blamed the further it took me from choosing thoughts of forgiveness and love. Time here has been a great healer, yet it was my excuse, when I thought so negatively. I never had enough time, I was always busy, running physically and emotionally away from others and myself.

Gradually learning to love and trust one significant other person who was willing to grow and respect me, helped me to say, "yes" to have children. My fear was that I could not be a 'good parent.' Gradually I realised I could break the old cycle and learn through reading and being around people who I respected as parents. The more honest I became with me the more I could be real with our children. I know I have lots to do in this area of being a parent and John Pollards Book "SELF-PARENTING" is helping me in the process of understanding me in relation to my outer children. I talk about this in chapter 6.

WORKING AS A TEAM

Linda and I work as a team, working as man and wife and as therapists. Most of our clients have been abused mentally, and physically. We work with a small group of committed counsellors. We have dedicated the past ten years to helping people plant seeds of love into their tortured lives. Plus challenge them as we challenge and grow ourselves, an ongoing process. I deeply respect Linda's approach to the healing process of growth. We are blessed with friendships and a rich community life. Every day I give thanks for our blessings.

OUT OF SADNESS CAME A BLESSING

A year ago Alex, my special buddy died in the arms of one of his clients. We trained together as counsellors. This shocked me, I wrote this to read at his memorial celebration.

To my soul brother-Alex.

Dear Alex, my friend who I love.
Even in your exchange from this life to another greater life, you have and still give me what it means to live life and be human in body, mind and soul. Thank you Alex for giving love to me and teaching me with your soul, your sense of fun, your free child, your eyes of compassion. When you taught me to windsurf my inner child leapt with your cheeky child. Thank you for being so patient with me. You helped me change my thoughts from fear to a love for the sea, wind and waves. You would teach me songs like "Fly Like an Eagle" as we skipped on the water and surged in the arms of the wind. Alex you touched so many minds and souls. We hardly talked about our work; our time was meant for playing with our

free child. When you or I saw the trees move one of us would ring the other and shout:

"Are you coming sailing?"

My excitement at you wanting to play with me was like nothing I had experienced before. When we met, we'd hug a great bear hug and rub our stubby beards. The light in your eyes was a sign to get the boards off the car and like two trainee Buddhists go through a meditation of "rigging up". We were the same lanky size and height, so we would swap boards and both being competitive would race around Pugneys Lake. If I won, you'd knock me off my board and we'd roar with laughter. If you won, you'd apologise, then grin with glee! We weren't competitive were we Alex?

In your presence, you gave me the chance to touch a power source from the universal mind. I believe you are now at one with that source. Living now with memories of you is sometimes painful and the tears come. Yet the pain is cleansed by the whisper of your angel. Alex I know you were no angel yet your struggle to be real, your many talents, your passion, your voice, your truth, your life is next door to my soul.

I love you Alex. Until our next windsurf in the heavenly skies.

Roger.

A week after Alex's death I was in the local library and a tape turned up in my hand "You Can heal Your Life" by Louise Hay. I intuitively knew to play it. I cried and cried for the loss of my friend and what I wanted to share with him. I knew about Louise years previously, yet had not been open to learning. I was not ready for my teacher. Now I was ready to move on, somehow I knew there was a blessing in Alex's sudden death; it was like a loving kick inside my soul to wake up. This reminds me what my old Buddhist trainer once said, "Wake up Roger and stop feeling sorry for yourself!" So for the past year I have studied and listened to tapes of so many writers on "How to love yourself?" Finding a place of deep respect within me and not feel guilty, about learning to love the miracle that we truly are.

This has been crucial to not being swayed by well meaning people who often want you to stay the same, for their own reasons. The impact on my family, friends, and wider community is still reverberating through life. My mother who is 84 has started to listen to tapes by Louise and finds she is learning how to see her life differently. As I have sent love and forgiveness to all my family we have began a deep healing and reconciliation process. One huge lesson for me is to clean up how I thought about my family. I can now talk to each of the family with genuine love and not just impatience and bitterness. I really don't want to write a poem "IF ONLY". This is a poem written by Erma Brook. This was written after she found she was dying of cancer.

IF I HAD MY LIFE TO LIVE OVER
(The spelling and grammar is how it came to me)

"If I had my life to live over I would have gone to bed when I was sick

Instead of pretending the earth would go into a holding pattern if I weren't there for the day.

I would have burned the pink candle sculpted like a rose before it melted in storage.

I would have talked less and listened more.

I would have invited friends over to dinner, even if the carpet was stained or the sofa faded.

I would have eaten the popcorn in the " good living" room and worried much less about the dirt when someone wanted to light a fire in the fire place.

I would have taken time to listen to my Grandfather ramble on about his youth.

I would have shared more of the responsibility carried by my husband.

I would have never insisted the car window be rolled up on a summer day because my hair had just been sprayed.

I would have sat on the lawn with my grass stains.

I would have cried and laughed less when watching television and more while watching life.

I would never have bought anything just because it was practical, wouldn't soil or was guaranteed to last a lifetime.

Instead of wishing away my nine months pregnancy I'd have cherished every moment and realised that the wonderment growing inside me was the only chance in life to assist God in a miracle.

When my kids kissed me impetuously, I would never of said, "later. Now get washed up for dinner."

There would have been more "I Loves you's". More I'm sorry's.

But mostly given another shot at life I would seize every minute look at it and really see it- live it and never give it back. Stop sweating at the small stuff. Don't worry about who doesn't like you, who has more, or who's doing what.

Instead lets cherish the relationships we have with those who do love us.

Lets think about what God has blessed us with and what we are doing each day to promote ourselves mentally, physically and emotionally.

I hope you all have a blessed day."

THE GROWING MIRACLE THRIVES IN LOVE

This for me sums up the need to learn to love ourselves that conveys a positive, caring and deep respect for the life we have been given. When I hold my Grandson I sense the miracle that we are. Now I want to help each person to come to that realisation and I cannot do it for you. We are each a miracle and let's use the power wisely. If this small book helps then lets celebrate and send more love into the world. Ask yourself; "What are your thoughts right now and whom are you joining with right now?" Thank you for reading part of my story.

Remember WHATEVER YOU PUT OUT COMES BACK MULTIPLIED.

And so it is.

Part II
Recognising & Overcoming the Blocks

CHAPTER 4
Anger & Guilt

"Whatever we believe becomes true for us."
Louise Hay

Anger and guilt are two barriers to loving the miracle that wants to unfold inside us. Imagine cutting off the sun and rain to a young flower plant; it would die or grow in a very crippled way. Most people have felt anger and guilt, both can produce punishment, pain and dis-ease if not recognised and expressed healthily. For some of us it can become a nightmare to express 'old' anger without enormous guilt and fear. A client who was abused repeatedly as a child by a relative in the family will often say something like this:

"If I get angry, I will lose control. I am not safe. I will hurt someone! I can't tell my parents, it would hurt them too much if I told them what happened! I know I am 40 years old but I feel like 6 years old".

This seesawing talk reflects the thoughts of a person who is beginning to express feelings of old anger. Instead of keeping feelings down, "old" anger comes up after years of being "stuffed" down (resentment), they are hitting memories from the past, and can trigger into panic with guilt very quickly. Yet anger is such a natural and normal emotion, my seven-month grandson gets furious if his needs aren't met, and once those needs are met he's radiating love again. Adults who have suppressed secret anger for years, due to fear and guilt, require very safe environments to express these feelings safely. Anger taken in and swallowed time and time again creates dis-ease in any part of our temple. The angry inner self-talk is often followed by immediate guilt; the beliefs become rigid, with layer upon layer of buried anger turned into resentment. These layers reflect the beliefs our parents and others had about us. A person who has never told anybody what went on in their childhood can build an extremely angry inner parent just like our own outer parents. In sessions an abused person can get in a rage at me acting out their scared inner child. Then they get to see how damaging their inner conversations are and why they were stuck. I talk later about building a loving inner parent. It is a vital step to real healing.

HEALTHY WAYS TO EXPRESS ANGER

If you cannot express anger to the person directly, for any reason, they are dead, not being believed, or you choose that it's not appropriate; you can do any of the following:

• Find a good therapist who will guide and help you unpack the unexpressed rage, if you have experienced deep habitual anger from being violated or are in an abusive relationship.

• Get in a car and go somewhere safe and scream (I have done this many times when working on my anger).

• Get a rolling pin and hit the bed. Make sure you're safe. Listen to your body and it will tell you what you're angry about. Get some clay and mould your thoughts and feelings. Then let your figures speak to you.

• Bite a cushion or pillow; so much anger is in our face and jaw.

• Lie on your bed and rant like a child kicking your legs.

• Throw cushions at someone you trust and shout "NO".

• Buy a boxing bag, put it up in your room and hit it.

• Go and play a game vigorously, without hurting you or your opponents.

• Join a voice workshop and let your voice become heard. I am just listening to Jill Rakusen, a wonderful voice workshop leader sing " WE CAN BREAK THE CHAIN OF ANGER" in a song called 'The Time Has Come to Sing a Song of Love'.

• Join an assertive training group, read any book by Gael Lindenfield: learn to assert yourself.

• Get a bunch of old magazines and rip them to shreds, or with old pillows.

• If you don't know what you're angry at be patient and let your body tell you as you hit pillows. Your body won't lie!

Louise Hay suggests MIRROR WORK in her book "You Can Heal Your Life". This is one of the most helpful, yet not easy ways I have found to express my anger constructively. I sit in front of a big mirror and have a list of whom I am angry with and tell them exactly what I am thinking and feeling. At first I found this hard, looking into my own eyes, I could not lie to my soul. I would think of any excuse, even cleaning the toilet was better than facing people I was angry towards. Yet with me encouraging others to do this exercise I knew I had to work through my anger. Once I started and I looked into my own eyes whole areas of memory came into my conscious mind about each person, then the tears and deep grief came and I started to talk to the person about my anger at them. Then the most surprisingly healing part was saying "I forgive you," in a growl at first, then I just carried on repeating "I forgive you and myself, I set you and me both free," and I often end the session saying, "what I really wanted was your love and approval." So often this is what we really want from the person we are so angry with. Later I would walk in the country and shout out "I am free and you are free." My dog Buddy would look at me kind of lopsided, yet with total unconditional love. You may say this is indulgent, let that resistance go, you have been so angry, you find wonderful reasons why to avoid your old anger.

Remember underneath anger there may be grief, the sadness of what wasn't there, like a parent saying "I love you and I am here for you." it may give room for healing tears to come.

FEAR OF MAKING A NOISE

Often noise is such an inhibitor for a person, if there were threats given to you like "I'll kill you if you make a noise", it may be so hard to let the growl, the noise of your own voice through. A bioenergetic exercise is helpful; when you stand up, open your legs and let the top part of your body fall forward at the same time letting out your breath. Let your arms chop the air as your head comes down, do this each day, and just notice what happens. There is such a need in communities for safe rooms, where people could go into a sound proof room, to let off steam! I believe this would prevent so much violence in all ages and the predisposition for becoming addicted. Anger expressed healthily and safely can reduce abuse, self-harming, road rage, and domestic violence. Taking responsibility for our anger is a vital ingredient to reducing blame and opening us to love and forgiveness, plus deep compassion.

To go further I try to help a client source their anger yet not indulge in being angry, moving on and growth is the goal. I am always seeking intelligent and practical ways old anger can become healed? One lovely idea is to learn to garden and clear a small patch of ground and dig all the old weeds out and care for that with love, then plant the seeds and shrubs you want. When I am in the garden I am beginning to think and see more clearly. Something really beautiful happens when you start digging. My partner loves to garden, I can always tell if she has been in the garden. I know both my parents love to garden, gardening is a wonderful therapy!

SEEING THE NEGATIVE INDICATORS OF ANGER AND GUILT

Some indicators of anger and guilt being present, which attracts some bizarre ways anger seeps out into our body, life and relationships.

- Overeating or under-eating, often feeling sick if you do get slightly angry.

- Being accident-prone small or large. A client has just had a car accident, as he is hitting a lot of memories of his abuse, luckily nobody was hurt.

- Getting into fights! When I lived in New Zealand, every Friday night was a night in the post office (pub) to get drunk and pick a fight-a poor male way of expressing anger, which has now spread to women in nightclubs.

- Crying all the time and wanting to hurt yourself.

- Being irritated with others, often gossiping and blaming others.

- Impatience with yourself and constant analysing.

- The words you speak are so powerful; if you swear and curse you attract experiences that reflect your inner and outer conversations.

- Unwilling or feeling unable to learn.

- Authoritarian thinking and behaviour where anger pervades like a threat, you feel it only needs a trigger and the person will erupt. I often have male clients who bristle with anger in the early stages of counselling. Punch bags can be a safe way to exhaust the scolding inner parent. Recently a physically strong woman, who came as a total victim to her mother's criticism, hit the bag so hard she lifted me off my feet while I held it. It is marvellous to see a person own their anger safely and dissolve so much fear and guilt. Resentment, anger turned in on yourself is a killer, a poison waiting to be released inside every cell of your body. I often see more mature people riddled with unexpressed anger, criticising everybody and ending up ill and unwilling to learn.

- Old people's homes often house tormented souls; this does not have to be. And when you listen deeply to elderly people a story erupts of a child that felt unloved. It is never too late to love yourself and let go the barriers to living your life with some inner peace and the divine presence guiding you. Healing miracles then happen, it's like our deep heart intention is heard and felt by our maker and the intelligence that made us, who gives life back abundantly, believe it.

Today I have received such confirmation of this from a man who was so angry, who had lost everything-wife, children and business, his hatred, anger and guilt poured from him. Life was going to end at the end of a rope. He made a deep decision to change and did everything I suggested and more, a year down the road of life he is being blessed, now even when life is tough he gives thanks and learns the lesson. He is beginning to be far more honest with himself; this is a vital step to healing. Repressed anger is witnessed in the way we drive, so often people travel and drive with dangerous thoughts, they blame others for their bad driving then drive a few feet from the person in front of them at such dangerous speeds. The way we travel is so much a mirror to our own level of consciousness. I listen to positive tapes when I drive; this calms my thinking and protects me. One day I will write a book called *"Affirmations for your car!"*

CAN YOU STOP BEING ANGRY WITH YOURSELF?

Choose to change the way you talk inside and outside your head. This is why positive affirmations are so vital. We learn so much in the first months and years of our childhood about what is legitimate and what is not acceptable with difficult feelings such as anger. As you contemplate thoughts about anger and guilt just go within and let the presence of the divine intelligence guide you into dissolving anger and let go of all grudges. If you sit in false righteousness you will spread guilt to others and stay stuck, so let go.

THE BENEFITS

When we let go our guilt and anger we regain a real sense of humour. It is such a blessing to witness a person laughing like a child after so many years of pent up anger and guilt. I notice such an increase in a person's free emotional and creative intelligence when they release energy to where it is supposed to be. Their eyes shine, they change how they dress, colour comes back into everything and a child-like creativity joins the adult self. Healing energy of every kind is released and one huge burden is lifted, not having to explain yourself to anybody. Other people's opinions of you real or unreal no longer hold power in your life. You begin to think in your mind without guilt, a freedom that is a joy to experience.

EXERCISE

Ask some of the following questions to yourself.

1. How did your Mum and Dad or their substitutes express anger? For example: My mother would bang things down on the table and scowl. Then whoever was closest she would use cutting remarks, that scolded my inner child, so fear of anger from others, especially women was and still can collapse

my inner world. A woman yelling at me is my nightmare scenario, or blaming me. This is not healthy as I work and live with women, who are extremely angry with men, so layers in me still need working on. Seeing them is the first step then I can begin releasing old pent up anger, fear and guilt. My father would go white-faced and speak slowly and in a threatening manner. As children we are geniuses at picking up the cues of our parents or teachers. I never learnt that it was safe to have my anger, until I worked in primal workshops where I was safe to do womb work and do some re-birthing. Still I can't show anger at any father figures, without enormous feelings of guilt or fear, yet I am now not scared of my own power.

2. What did your sisters or brothers do with their anger? For example: My two sisters would have enormous arguments shouting and yelling from one part of the house to the other. They would then come and tell me how awful the other one was. Sometimes they took it out on me as I was the youngest and they would sit on me until I gave in. I became a safe place to dump anger, until I fought back. We now laugh at this.

3. Was one particular person blamed in the family for anything? At the meal tables considerable arguments or abusive comments can be directed to one or two in the family. Jokes at a child's expense in association with food can have enormous consequences. In one client, anorexia began when her father constantly made fun of her. It was not until she safely expressed her anger, at first with guilt of being disloyal, that a very free anger was expressed safely and this began her healing.

4. What did you do with your anger? As a child and as an adult, do you see any family pattern? One client would feel anger and stuff her face until she was sick, (Bulimia) then start eating again. After many sessions this lady expressed her anger safely around her mother who told her "she was not good enough at her school work" so she learnt to go to the cupboard and started eating. When she saw the connection and had her anger she stopped eating excessively. She now works abroad and is freer to express her intelligence and creativity.

5. What methods do you use to hold on to your anger? For me it was eating excessively, luckily I burned the excess weight quickly, or I would punish myself with long inner conversations, or get busy, clean the house from top to bottom! When I had a mixture of fear and anger I would go into the woods and shout hitting trees with sticks, then hug them afterwards. The woods became a second home for me when I was young. Now I go

out to sea and shout when windsurfing, I find this so therapeutic. As a counsellor to so many angry people, I need to find balance and renew my inner wisdom. I have found walking, yoga, meditation and prayer helpful as well as visiting my dietician regularly. The unconditional love of our family dog Buddy, who is barking as I write this, is a great healer and comfort. Many of my clients love to take him for a walk after sessions, to comfort their inner child. A pet asks so little from us yet gives so much.

A builder has just come to look at my attic; he asked me, *"What do you do?"* When he heard, he told me he had prostate cancer with three years to live. I asked him *"Are you willing to learn supplementary ways that can heal your body and mind that could aid the medical approach?"* He was and went away with tapes and books, he said, *" I have a six year old daughter to live for, I love life."* Just before he knocked, I had been thinking, "divine love heals our world." Coincidence maybe, yet whatever you put out in thought word and action comes back. I look forward to the next meeting with this man.

EXERCISE

Visualise your rage flowing out of your body and being soaked up by the earth. Then send love to the person you are angry with, talk with their angel. Visualise your love dissolving the conflict between you. Just repeat the word "FORGIVE" or "PEACE" or "LOVE". Remember you can easily have a sexual visualisation. Why not give yourself a gift of visualising harmony. This sounds like a paradox and it is, yet having your anger safely and then forgiving is so healing, include forgiving yourself. Remember that guilt always seeks punishment and punishment produces pain, let go and let love in.

Restate this affirmation as often as you unconsciously may think its opposite! So this thought becomes a lovely habit.

"It is safe to change.
I allow myself to express uncomfortable thoughts and feelings safely
and I let them go with love.
I am divinely guided and protected in all
that I think, say and do.
Everything works out for my highest good.

And so it is."

MEDITATION

"Learn to be silent.
Let your quiet mind listen and absorb."
Pythagoras. (580 B.C. - 500 B.C.)

"All man's miseries derive from not being
able to sit quietly in a room alone."
Blaise Pascal (1623-1662)

I took these quotes from 'Wisdom of the Ages' by Dr Wayne Dyer. I awoke at 4 this morning and did a simple meditation. I suggest you do this daily.

"On the in breath think FOR.
On the out breath think GIVE."

Each time your thoughts wander go back gently to 'FOR' on the in breath and 'GIVE' on the out breath.

Do this for 5 minutes to begin with.
Then increase the time, as you feel able.

Just become aware.

CHAPTER 5
Criticism & Fear

"Learning to love ourselves reduces fear and negative criticism."

A little note to you the reader. This is the hardest chapter for me to write because I know one of my biggest lessons in this life is to dissolve criticism and fear. Having said that I have created the experience of disaster, blocked drains, the computer crashing, whole chunks wiped off saved documents, gas leaks, arguments, and feeling ill! When you decide to change your experience of some barrier to you loving you, life may get worse for a while; it's like you produce exactly what you don't want, the subconscious is in rebellion against the positive messages you are consciously putting into the old files.

Learning to love the miracle you are and being all that you can be, can seem miles off, when your inner conversation is constantly picking at you, and you judge yourself unmercifully. My family pattern was built on cynical criticism; we as a family would laugh at people's foolish mannerisms and politicians were unmercifully criticised. This became an unconscious habit; I became a prisoner to a habit, which in turn attracted a lot of fear and critical people around me. I became frightened of being criticised. One huge event in my memory was looking a fool in front of the classroom when I could not remember my Latin verbs; I always came bottom of the class in Latin.

So for me criticism of others and myself has been one way I have protected myself and kept stuck in the past, impeding positive growth and change. My childhood fear of being criticised has attracted to me clients who have similar negative barriers to loving themselves. Comparing myself to others negatively has been such a power drain to my self worth. One sunny afternoon a shy man came into my hut and blurted out. "My wife says I should come because I am stuck and I am boring, if I don't change I am frightened our marriage will end." He then went on to describe himself in the following ways. *"I was never any good at school, I'm very quiet, I don't know how to be sociable and I have a very boring job. I am uneducated and I don't have any interests or hobbies."* As the first session developed he briefly described his story. The main theme was he had always compared himself unfavourably to his twin brother, who he described as "clever, sociable and bright." He was constantly told he was stupid and not bright and all he could do when he left school was a labouring job. This is where he was now, he had attracted to himself a clever and sociable partner where he always felt criticised and all he could see was a hopeless future, not a healthy way to carry on. As he talked the insight was, *"nobody has ever taken an interest in me including me!"* I replied *"Are you willing to change and grow?"* The answer came without hesitation *"yes"*. This working class man (his description) made a deep inner commitment to change and grow for himself, and not just for his wife.

He carried out the following:

1. Meditated each morning; this helped him think and see clearly about how he came to believe certain negative thoughts about himself. Before, his habit was to read newspapers, sit in front of the television and soak up negativity of every kind.

2. He listened to self-help tapes every day; on the way to work he put a tape in his Walkman and became willing to listen to positive thoughts about how the mind and body worked. He got an appetite to learn, he started to study and ask well thought out questions. He always arrived on time and shared what he was learning, and often said, "Why aren't we taught at school about how to use our mind and think thoughts that support our growth? Why are we taught just maths and history?" For a man who had labelled himself as 'not bright', he was finding the spark of intelligence that is there for all of us when we make our intention clear like "I am willing to change and grow".

3. So going to and from work he repeated his affirmations. He started to talk to work colleagues about what he was learning and gradually he lost his fear of ridicule by them and as he grew each one of his work mates

respected him. He lost all sense of being embarrassed, by thoughts, which before, seemed like a foreign language.

4. Each time he came I sensed his energy for life was increasing, it was like seeing a young child grow and re-root themselves in good soil, with all the elements to help reproduce life giving thoughts.

THE OUTCOME

• He realised this was a continuing process working on his growth and he could either make it fun or hard work. He chose to lighten up the more he valued his life and his talents.

• He noticed he had more energy; he listened to his wife, yet stood his ground.

• They made love with passion; they talked and understood each other more.

• They joined dancing classes together and began to enjoy each other's company.

• He watched less TV and sport and enjoyed reading books that helped him understand himself and relationships.

• He realised he "deserved the best and not to just get by". This seems ideal, it was hard work and at times confronting, and he saw when and how he put himself down.

Each day he learnt to love himself a little bit more, after six months he said. "I don't need to come anymore and I know where you are. I know I am responsible for my mind, my life, and my experiences". I salute his willingness to learn, he certainly taught me to start letting go of my fear of being criticised.

GENETIC OR LEARNED?

So many of us have been brought up in an atmosphere of judgment and criticism, where making ourselves wrong and frightened seems like "second nature". It is not our "first nature" to constantly put ourselves down. Our first nature is to love the miracle we are, just watch a baby! It is not in our genes to be critical! I often ask people who are highly critical, "Where do you spend most of your thinking and feeling time?" Then I draw this well-known triangle. Susan Jeffers puts it succinctly in the following quote: "*If there is hell on earth, living as a victim with feelings of anger and blame defines it. If there is heaven on earth, living powerfully and lovingly as the creator of our own lives defines it*".

Most people see themselves in the victim role, and with a little further discussion they see how they move round the triangle extremely quickly, and often get into persecuting (blaming) others and then want to rescue or be rescued. This type of thinking feeling pattern creates fear and co-dependent behaviour, where the person continually wants to be reassured that they are loved, yet no matter how much they receive love from others, they cannot believe anybody can love them. Read "Women Who Love Too Much" by Robin Norwood, a life-changing book!

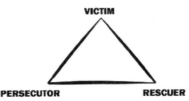

Do you see yourself on this triangle? Then write specific relationships that reflect your thinking for example: I often saw myself as a victim to other peoples negative opinions of me especially at work when I was a social worker. I had no boundaries I attracted to me people who didn't respect themselves or me. Violence and abuse was nearly a daily occurrence. I never thought I had the power to get out of the triangle.

FEAR OF CRITICISM REDUCES OUR WILLINGNESS TO LEARN
To ask a person to stop criticising him or herself is like changing a whole internal world of negative thinking. It can be done when you help the person talk and gradually see what negative ways they have built for survival. Nobody can be condemned for learning to judge and criticise, when they have accepted the opinions of others who themselves were so critical. The new beginnings of recognising and releasing our fears and critical thoughts and old beliefs that hurt you, is a continuous process.

In a group, I expressed how negative criticism makes a person retreat inside; it reduces the soul and can reduce our ability to learn from our higher intelligence. I was told, "It's the only way we can progress and grow." If this is our daily experience then what we keep attracting to ourselves, is more criticism. Often those who are most critical of others, attract to them much to be critical of. Constructive feedback given with well thought out ideas and listening creates such a different environment.

Carl Rogers wrote a superb book on "Student centred learning". This changed my whole approach to what a teacher and student can accomplish together. I often see a negative attitude in leaders, who come from the old school of "hit out before you're hit" politicians, teachers and medical hierarchy. It can often be seen in religious leaders who vent their inner fury onto the passive congregation. This can lead people to interpret God as a punishing God. So the inner fear and guilt can grow in an already guilt ridden audience. The inner child is again feeling scolded by parental figures.

WHAT THOUGHTS ARE YOU SENDING TO YOUR SUBCONSCIOUS MIND NOW?

When we choose such critical thoughts we are sending messages of self-punishment to our whole subconscious mind and body, to every cell and organ. However when we choose to say loving, positive thoughts to our self, our body, mind and spirit will respond in a healing and creative way. We are far from PERFECT; I have just experienced how critical I can be in my own inner conversations. One little challenge after another happened this weekend. The sink got blocked, took it apart, and then with great difficulty put it together. After this the outside drain got blocked, spent 2 hours with my arms in muck! Followed by the computer emailing system crashing. Then just as we get into bed, we luckily found a gas leak hissing from the main pipe. Then as I meditated this morning I just asked, *"What is it I need to learn?"* And I saw how I was overloading myself with pressure; some might call stress, which I re-interpret as making myself frightened and critical. What was the universe trying to tell me?

Writing this first book I am learning how I can make myself feel wrong. Statements like, *"nobody will read this, and publishers will reject it, am I coming from the right intention?"* So as my thinking got increasingly negative on the inside the more my outer experiences got blocked. This in turn affected the whole family in how we planned the weekend. Then just as I was sitting down to type this chapter on "criticism and fear", I nearly convinced myself I am not feeling well, so I go to bed and sleep. On waking I think and started to say, *"I am feeling awful"*. Then with my free will I said, "I am thinking clearly in my world". Followed by the thought *"put on a lovely tape and relax!"* My reality hummed with fresh energy. I chose to change my thoughts.

POSITIVE TIPS

I awoke this morning with deep critical thoughts, so straight to the mirror looking pretty unsightly, I mumbled "I love you Roger. What can I do to make you happy?" The answer was unrepeatable to begin with, yet the thought came to "go and meditate and then talk with my inner child". So I meditated, then I went and sat in the chair and had a written conversation with my inner child, who revealed a lot of anger at the inner parent. The early morning for me and I suspect many millions of people, reveals our thoughts and feelings at their most negative. I often listen to a positive meditation tape first thing in the morning. My children used to suffer it at first, now if I haven't got a tape on they want to know why? What's that saying about our mind absorbing good habits, children love to hear and speak good things if you give them the chance. Remember this tip. Have your affirmations of what you want to achieve put up on mirrors, walls and anywhere in your space. I have them by my computer as I type, for example:

*DIVINE WISDOM GUIDES AND PROTECTS ME
IN ALL MY WRITING.*

*I HAVE WONDERFUL RELATIONSHIPS AT HOME, WORK
AND PLAY.*

I AM IN THE PROCESS OF POSITIVE CHANGE.

I LOVE AND APPROVE OF MYSELF.

I AM SAFE, IT'S ONLY CHANGE.

I AM A MIRACLE.

*I AM OPEN AND RECEPTIVE TO ALL GOOD AND MY
INCOME IS CONTINUALLY INCREASING.*

I LOVE MY MIND.

I NEVER LOSE BY LOVING.

I AM IN THE RIGHT PLACE AT THE RIGHT TIME.

AS I SAY YES TO LOVE, LOVE SAYS YES TO ME.

*THE MORE I FORGIVE THE MORE I SET MYSELF FREE AND
ALL THOSE I FORGIVE, I SET THEM FREE.*

I AM GOOD ENOUGH.

I LET GO OF ALL NEED TO CRITICISE.

As you read this write your affirmations now, get some paper or cards and put them up where you will see them. My friend Karen has a brilliant idea, by putting *"I now intend to open the door of possibilities by...."* and you write what you want to do. See her website www.possibilitiesinaction.com So when you are at your most delightfully negative, you look at those thoughts unconsciously and this helps your subconscious mind choose thoughts that dissolve the negative. You may say this is false, yet think how often you have used energy in your temple, your mind, to choose negative. Give yourself a "gift" of choosing not to beat yourself up.

This has been a life changer for me. It is not "psuedo positive it's creative thinking." When you are at your most vulnerable, I am not saying you deny your feelings, you thank those thoughts and feelings for sharing and you just say in your mind "*I DESERVE TO CHOOSE WHAT I REALLY WANT, NOT WHAT I HAVE BEEN PROGRAMMED TO THINK IN THE PAST*". For me this has become fun after a long period of having huge considerations of feeling brain washed. I used to argue with my Buddhist teacher who would laugh at me gently, at how I created and attracted to myself a hard way up the mountain of life.

Last night I sat with my friend and we just shared from the heart; he was a client, now he is a great friend. Just being with somebody when you both listen to each other with unconditional love can be like nectar to the soul. I have often been a loner and prided myself with that, now as I value me I truly value my friends. To relax with somebody, laugh out loud, cry with him or her, share the intimate secrets and find they often feel or think the same is so healing. It can shift our energy to be with real friends even when they are down.

GOSSIP

One area engages my critical self; this is when I talk about somebody behind their back. Each time I do this, I ask myself "Would I like this said about me?" The answer is "no," now I value me. Before I could easily criticise and gossip. Watch what comes out of your mouth, conversations can so easily move into gossip and critical judgments. You can probably think right now of ways you state your "put downs". When you gossip how do you feel? What are you doing to change this? When I gossip, I now ask myself, "What is it in me that's attracting this to me?" When I go within I see more clearly, criticism and gossip keeps you negatively attached to the person you're belittling and attracts further negative fear and criticism to yourself.

SEEING OUR BARRIERS DISSOLVE BY WORKING ON YOURSELF IN A SELF- EMPOWERMENT GROUP

I have just returned from a group where 30 people were learning to love who they are. The benefits of listening and sharing in a group far out weigh the negative, if you come from an intention of love. Each time I help facilitate self-empowerment groups, I sense there is a presence that is larger than the whole. A healing energy is released when groups come together to change and grow, with the goal and process of learning to love who we are. I just give thanks for the insights, growth, changes and the honesty in such groups. Subscribe to www.positivenews.net. This has news of economic, social and practical progress and reduces our tendency to listen to negative news. The articles connect us to people who are working practically on real issues in every part of the earth. DO IT NOW. I promise you it will help your growth to listen and read news that is made by people like you and me, who are changing their lives positively, practically, spiritually and economically.

As I finish this chapter I give thanks for all my friends and family who have loved me while I write this book. I am slowly learning to overcome my fears of rejection and value me as I am.

Please answer these as honestly as you can.

1. In what ways did your father criticise you? Did you learn fear and in what way? (Or those who substituted for your parents).

2. What did you learn about self-criticism and fear from your mother?

3. How did your mother (or substitute) criticise you and what about?

4. In what ways did the family judge each other?

5. Can you remember the first time you were criticised at school and how did that develop throughout school? What were your teachers telling you? What did you fear at school?

Be as honest as you can, please don't beat yourself up as you see the patterns.

EXERCISE
Just experiment now with the following two contrasting thoughts and say them out loud. Open your arms wide and preferably in front of a mirror: *"I am an open and receptive channel for divine ideas to flow through me now."* Go on put your arms out wide. Note how you feel? Then say, *"I am a victim and I fear doing anything wrong."* You will probably fold your arms. How do you think and feel now?

CHAPTER 6

Creating a Positive Inner Parent to Love our Inner Child

"Loving the inner child helps you love yourself and life"
My inner child said that

Many of us have a lost feeling and creative girl or boy inside us that needs a loving inner parent. So many apparently grown men and women come to my little garden hut, complaining about their relationships. Sometimes it seems, *"Men are from Mars and Women are from Venus"*, John Gray. As a male I was brought up in a male dominated emotionally arrested family and culture. I often suspected there was an ingredient missing from my parents. This was a genuine inner and outer language of love within my parents for who they were. Often I will ask a client *"Were you ever told you were loved?"* The answer comes *"no never"* in such a manner that I should even ask.

At school, I found the same ingredients of a loving encouraging language missing from teachers and as I moved through my life I found this ingredient missing in me and in many people I met. In fact I seemed to attract people who had a hurt inner child. "Life is a mirror." I learnt that people did not love themselves, especially their inner child. Not only could my parents not understand each other, there was in both of them an arrested (stuck) feeling emotional child within them trying to be loved and understood, plus a very critical inner parent that they had internalised from their parents. It was like generations of unloved inner children coming down to parent my child. Their parents were coming from such "unloving homes" and so on down the line. I twigged this rather late in the day that I was being parented by two adult children who were sometimes emotionally younger than I was. My parents could not show deep emotional love to me, that they never received from their parents. My parents truly did the best with what they knew. Now I love and understand them as two individuals who are so much happier and in separate relationships that they enjoy and are free to be themselves. When I am listening to a "grown" woman or man talk about their bad marriage or relationship, I often detect an unloved inner baby, child and teenager that is emotionally crying out to be appreciated, listened too, understood and loved. If you are emotionally at 5 or 10 and you're in the body of a 40-year-old, it is hard to have passionate sex or hold down a responsible job or write coherent essays for an academic course. It's like whole chunks of personal and social development are missing. In this chapter I want to help you acknowledge your inner child, and then provide some suggestions to help you positively re-parent your inner child.

INTERNALISED PARENT AND CHILD

We all have an internalised parent and child within us, if you listen to your inner conversations enough you will discern gradually one voice is a parent, with all its mood swings, the other voice is your inner child with all its mood swings. You learnt this by the age of about seven and probably before all the main thought and feeling patterns (beliefs) about yourself from all the significant adults. Now if your outer parents were negative to your child, you in turn may do the same to your inner child as you grow in age. We can be 50 years old and yet feel emotionally about 8 years old and respond in that manner, especially when our needs for being loved and nurtured are not being met.

Often memories from an unloved childhood will re- surface when we enter a serious relationship and more so when we become a real parent. If it is true that our self-image is created by the way adults treated us in our early years, our own children can then trigger our own childhood memories, often with a negative consequence. The screams of a baby can panic a young mother into complete confusion, the cry of her own inner baby or child is screaming back. If we learnt that nobody was there for us emotionally when we were young, it is extremely hard for us to be there for our children, as a positive encouraging and motivating parent. As I write this it is Boxing Day and how often I hear grown adults say, *"I dread seeing my parents because I can't be me!"* Holidays like Christmas are often mini-nightmares for the families, where memory 'buttons' get pushed with little real awareness of what is being played out. Unmet social and creative needs in our life can create a deep emotional void, where an adult is unable to communicate fun, love and energy due to a childhood of being over criticised.

THE LOST CHILD

For many adults who have an inner child that continually criticises itself is like feeling a foreign being inside you which nobody understands including you the lost lonely child that nobody loved including your inner scolding parent. Often in therapy I witness a grown person still carrying a highly critical parent and/or frightened rebellious child. The venom and rage from the child that was never heard and the internalised parent that never stops blaming can do enormous damage to a person making successful steps towards loving him or herself. To help change this I create a safe environment, where hopefully the child can feel believed, understood and given some basic listening with unconditional love. Then I encourage the person to move on to reading books like "SELF-PARENTING" by John K Pollard 111. This one book has the simplest yet deeply healing exercises for your inner parent allowing your inner child to express its thoughts and feelings in a daily structured way. I recommend this book.

By using John Pollards self-parenting methods, your inner parent can learn to positively love and genuinely nurture your inner child. Both inner child and parent can become allies using talents and skills together. It's like the right and left-brain come together and you re-wire them. Our genius "wonder child" can safely appear, grow and thrive, without being scolded! Do also read "Homecoming" by John Bradshaw.

We all have inner conversations you are having one right now. Do you ever say to yourself "I am just like my mum" and you vowed you wouldn't be when you grew up, well that is a direct reflection on your inner conversations. An example of an inner conversation and how inner blame can work to keep you stuck in your daily outer experiences.

(C= inner child   P= inner parent)

C -   *"I hate work!"*

P -   *"We have to go to work to make money."*

C -   *"I'm fed up of work."*

P -   *"Me too! But if we make more money we can start a business."*

C -   *"You say that every time."*

P -   *"That's not true."*

C -   *"I want to have some fun in my life let's go windsurfing".*

P -   *"Shut up, get real."*

C -   *"You shut up!"*

Conclusion conflict and no win for both parties. Often a person will arrive saying in a hurt child voice *"I hate my job and partner and I can't see what to do"*. This often shows me there is a negative inner conversation continually going on in this adult, which makes everything wrong. John Pollard suggests when we write these inner conversations each day we get to see what we are thinking and why we keep going in circles. The idea is to get a win/win situation. Let me replay that dialogue with an encouraging listening inner parent and a creative child.

C -   *"I'm fed up with work!"*

P -   *"Thanks for sharing that. What could we do to change our lives?"*

C -   *"Go windsurfing."*

P -   *"Thanks, yes we could do that. What else could we do to enjoy work?"*

C -   *"Well you have always wanted to write."*

P -   *"Thanks yes, but am I too old and would anybody buy what I want to write?"*

C -   *"You can do anything you set your mind to that's what you tell me."*

P -   *"Thanks you're my best pal!"*

C -   *"Lets get up early and start writing."*

P -   *"What will we write about?"*

C -   *"I'll give you plenty of ideas I love just being playful and creative."*

P -   *"Lets look forward to a great partnership."*

Here the parent listens and encourages the child to come up with ideas. The child remembers what the parent and adult always wanted to do and encourages the parent when they doubt themselves. I love doing these inner dialogues daily you get to see how creative and loving you can become. Then life gets a whole lot better.

NO-LIMITS

When we create a loving inner parent and a creative inner child, I find the following benefits:

- You do not impose on each other you listen and encourage.
- The child feels safe to play with ideas and feelings. You love to learn

new ideas by reading and listening and find new creative avenues in work and pleasure.

• You can do these written inner dialogues anywhere; it's best to do them for 30 minutes a day.

• You become easy to be around, at home and work. Your own children or children in general will feel safer and more playful. As I write this in my son's bedroom, I have kids playing and laughing around me, they have just asked me "What are you typing"? I told them; one young boy replied, "I talk to myself all the time it helps me not to feel scared especially at school".

• My son is a natural soul at making friends and playing. He shows me how to use his lap top computer! Before I wrote this book I was scared of computers, now with my children's help and my inner child being willing to learn, I love playing on my "magic toy".

• As you re-parent yourself with a loving inner dialogue you will see those close to you with new eyes.

• Your approach to change will become enthusiastic.

• You will take time out to play and rest.

• Goals become mutually agreed between your inner child and parent and those close to you, so far less conflict.

• You model positive inner conversations so outer relationships reflect that and you enjoy new challenges. People "get a positive buzz" off you rather than take from you and you stop being a drain on other people.

TALK TO YOUR INNER "WONDER" CHILD DAILY
You're inner child will intuitively help you if you start affirming her or him, each morning go to the mirror and say to your inner child:

> *"I love you and I am here for you. What can I do to make you happy today?"*

Then listen and be patient a forgotten child may be silent or just be cynical at first. Then do what the child wants; it can be in your imagination. I often visualise taking my child to the beach just playing, paddling and chucking a ball. Just enjoy being there for your "wonder child" (John Bradshaw). One day my inner creative child thought up the affirmations in this book. Just after I had asked him in the mirror *"What would you like to do today?"* The answer came, "write some positive affirmations about me." So I sat down and wrote them they just came naturally. Then I put out an affirmation to meet a wonderful loving illustrator, three days later John Welding came into my life, now we are like two creative children. Did I have a critical parent that said, " You can't write affirmations, nobody will want to read them?" Yes that came, however I sensed my inner child was listened too by my higher self, my nurturing inner power, which slowly builds a loving inner parent that I always wanted as a child. While I type this, a talented pianist is playing beautiful music on our old piano he composed this piece last week after talking with his inner child. For many years he has hated himself and consequently became depressed, he now loves playing the piano it allows him to feel he can excel in what he loved as a child, his "wonder" child thrives at the piano. I know he can translate this to everyday relationships. (A year after the above was written I went to his first solo concert, he surprised everyone with his skill and passion.)

EMOTIONAL VOIDS
When a thirty-year-old mum says. "When my son wants me to play with him, I can't, I want to, but then I lose my temper or I find something else to do." This is a cry from the heart; I have been there myself! I ask, "Were you ever played with?" The answer comes like a bullet "NO, they never had time!" The deep well of angry pain comes to the surface and here begins the real story of their childhood. It's like you have nothing to go to inside yourself; all you feel is helpless and then you get angry at what you really want to love. The cycle of panic and extreme anxiety can then set in and without an inner parent and a partner that's reassuring, you can feel powerless. Again seek and affirm that the right people and support are coming to you now. Say this right now.

> *"I am open and receptive to a new awareness, a raising of my consciousness of who I am and I build loving relationships within and without that help me love myself, all parts of me."*

With this intention the universal mind will bring you the support you need. So often in my healing the right person, book, tape and just a friend phoning at the right time has helped me. I find in my counselling of clients they have taught me so much about myself and given me a gift of insights to myself. When I am transparently me and open to the healing process of deep soul talk, just witnessing another persons healing is a privilege.

TWO PEOPLE DARING TO BE REAL TO THEMSELVES AND EACH OTHER

When couples come for counselling and they understand each other's childhood, a quiet healing miracle can be seen in the following ways:

• They start to allow each other to be a child and not be embarrassed. If the feeling boy or girl is safe enough to emerge, so much healing and genuine love can grow.

• Both sexes take on new softer and stronger parts of their real identity; they balance their masculine and feminine energies.

• Each owns their feelings and takes sensitive responsibility for them.

• They validate themselves and each other and can start believing positive affirmations from their inner child.

• Their sex life becomes part of a healing process. They listen to each other's needs, and if sex is mutually desired, then a special intimacy is built from their playful and loving child. (I often want to just be held when my inner baby surfaces during lovemaking.)

• They want more knowledge on how to re-parent their inner child.

• They read books together and share their insights and reflections.

• They begin to have genuine patience and are far less critical of themselves, their partner and their own children.

DENIAL BY YOUR PARTNER

However when one partner is in denial and is blocked, the one who wants to change and learn to love all parts of their life can find it so hard. Often there is a gap that seems unbridgeable, many men and women exist in what I call "no person land". They live in a home where the inner and outer children witness and experience the hurt of two "grown-ups", (two adult children fighting). So often the man cannot contact his inner child in a loving way, he feels so threatened when the woman wants to talk about feelings. After the honeymoon, couples, heterosexual or homosexual can uncover unconsciously in themselves and in each other a hurt inner child that comes with a scolding critical parent. So BREAK THE CYCLE OF HURT AND PAIN. Ask yourself:

"WHAT'S THE GREATEST RISK, TO STAY THE SAME OR CHANGE?"

PERHAPS THE GREATEST RISK IS STAYING THE SAME!

SUGGESTIONS OF THINGS THAT I HAVE FOUND
HELP CLIENTS AND FRIENDS

Be prepared to change the thoughts you choose to think in your mind, without guilt. Learn about using your conscious mind to reprogram your subconscious mind.

• Remind yourself *"It is safe to change and grow"*. Say this repeatedly especially when you are fearful of change.

• Read books, (see list in the back), if you find reading hard listen to tapes, listen to positive tapes wherever you go, buy a Walkman.

• Talk with yourself in the mirror in a loving way every day. Pin up positive thoughts anywhere, I risk repeating myself yet we so often need that when our subconscious mind says, "that's not going to work."

• If you're in a partnership run the affirmation below through your mind whether your partner wants to grow or not. You can only send love to another person; don't manipulate them by telling them what they should do. We each have our own lessons to learn, you can't learn my lessons for me.

> *"With divine healing I send love to my partner.*
> *I send unconditional love to their inner child and*
> *I am learning to love the miracle of my life.*
> *I am learning to express abundant love happiness and joy*
> *in all areas of my life."*

• Remember you will make mistakes you are not perfect; just learn to love yourself a little step at a time. The universal mind will provide people, resources and new opportunities as your inner conversations become more loving and forgiving.

• As you make progress give thanks, so more good will come into your life. If you have children, talk with them openly about what you are learning; yes you may get some funny jibes, yet secretly they will love you for being in love with life.

• Children will love to be around you as you learn to love yourself without guilt and you dissolve the scolding inner parent, they will respond to your playful child.

• If you're single and want a partner, run this affirmation through your mind. Repeat as many times in the mirror, and note your resistance.

Love The Miracle You Are

"I am open and receptive to attracting to me a partner.
I am creating in me the qualities I want in my partner.
The creativity of the universe and its divine love is
bringing us together."

List the qualities you want in your partner and create them in yourself, this is a crucial step to finding a partner, so often we attract who we are critical of, because we expect others to change and make us happy.

• Remember as you work on becoming more conscious and positive you will be connecting to similar people on a "SOUL" level. I believe God; the universal creator will direct you to all the right people and places plus aid your decisions. You will choose to let go and let divine love express through you.

• Your inner child and a nurturing inner parent will become "allies" and this will help reduce inner conversations that put you down and others down.

• You will find that positive affirmations work, if you just keep doing them, in the most miraculous ways, please don't say, "I don't believe it" when something good happens. Just give thanks and give out more love to family and the people you pass in the street, pray positively for governments, send love and peace to places of conflict, and keep on forgiving.

• Your energy will increase and your spiritual life will blossom as you think clearly in your mind. Often stop during the day and say "I SEE CLEARLY" or "I THINK CLEARLY" and just watch what happens.

• Your words will change, you will think and speak words that are creative, giving life, healing, love, and joy. You will become a channel for the creativity of the universe to express itself through you. Each day will be an adventure, now is the only time.

• Your inner child and nurturing parent will help each other be creative in your work.

• Every area of your life will change, welcome this and let go of expectations, let the divine energy of love flow through you.

• Keep repeating I DESERVE LOVE; this is not selfish it will shine God; it is what we all deserve to re-connect to the miracle we are! As you learn your lessons on this planet, you will help others. Divine Love cannot be stopped, or kept a secret; this in turn will help heal our planet. And so it is.

Part III
Trusting the Power Within

CHAPTER 7
*Learning to Trust the Power & Presence That Made Us
& That's Within Us*

"Everything works out for our highest good"

As I write this book, three days ago my grandchild Louis was taken into hospital with meningitis, this is life threatening. The experience for Louis at 4 months, nobody can guess, to what he was feeling and what he may remember. As I phoned people to pray and I comforted mum and dad on that first night, the inner thought that came to me was "Everything will work out for Louis highest good." At first I became shocked and bitter as I drove through Leeds nearly running over a drunken man on that late Saturday night. Asking *"Why? Why? Why God?"* Lots of questions and old feelings of "Why Louis? - Just take me". Then while I held his hand at his cot in the intensive care ward, I experienced a deep peace inside me. It was at five in the morning, and all I could sense was a power of exceptional goodness and love being with Louis. You could say I imagined it, but I will never forget this power that can be present, when we really call on the higher self inside. I knew prayer was also coming from hundreds of people.

Some will call the power, Jesus, Holy Spirit, infinite source, Allah or God. You name your God what you will. All I experienced was something like an unseen presence just sending love into his body, past all the tubes, flashing lights and buzzers, nurses, and doctors. It was like a moment of time that stopped and a healing voice of love whispered love inside Louis. The whisper matched the soul beat of Louis's soul and somewhere gave me peace. We know that prayer is the greatest power on earth, so many people praying, yet it was like I was witnessing such a natural healing love, the presence surpassed all understanding with the rational thinking mind.

With a heart felt feeling of thanks to that unseen healing love, Louis has made a full recovery, and my thanks to the dedicated doctors and nurses and all who work in hospitals. What was amazing was the right people came at the right time and contributed to his healing, even somebody I had negative judgments about, was exactly the right person to find a vein in Louis' chubby foot to put in the tube for the antibiotics. My affirmation as I sat with my daughter and son-in-law was: *"Send the right help at the right time and the right people to heal my grandson. Give them inner guidance and protect us all with your divine love. And so it is Amen"*.

WHEN LIFE GETS TOUGH LEARN THE LESSONS

Believe me when I say it is the greatest gift to learn to love from deep within you and you find that deep inner presence, for me it is a loving and healing God. Sometimes when I meditate I sense this presence or when I sit quietly with someone who needs healing. It really is a peace that goes beyond the physical. Learning to love and dissolve the past barriers to loving the miracle you are, building your consciousness of this presence is a journey worth learning and living.

Healing comes in strange ways as Louis has been in hospital. My past has loomed large, yet not with criticism, especially around my first marriage. As I sat with my present wife and ex-wife (who were both wonderful in their acceptance and wisdom of each other) it was like parts of me coming together. For me it was like finding pieces of a jigsaw puzzle and knowing where to put them in the picture of my life so far. To serve my daughter and son in law was a gift. I benefited from the gift of love they returned to me. Thank you.

GOING BEYOND THE PAIN

Shared pain can be healing, don't run away from learning "Your highest Good" can be served by tough events in your life. Approaching a painful experience with love I believe creates what Sanaya Rowan and Duane Packer say "Miracles come from love, are created by love and magnetized to you through love". Trusting that even in dark and difficult experiences the intention of thinking and saying "Only good will come out of this experience" immediately changes the energy.

A few weeks ago I was nearly involved in a pile up on the M1 motorway. When I drive now I always put in a positive affirmation tape (my university on wheels) this particular day my mobile telephone wasn't working before the accident. Luckily or a "God coincidence," I stopped at a service station and passed a telephone shop, they mended my phone while I ate. At the time I was reading a book, by Louise Hay. "The Power is Within You." An hour later, I was repeating in my mind: "*I am safe, I am surrounded by good drivers, and I am safe*". The next few seconds, a large German lorry caught a small white van in front of me; it dragged the van in front of the lorry into the inside lane. My first thought was to brake and the thought came, who is going to come into me? Luck, coincidence, or divine protection, nobody did. The white van came to a halt, I pulled up and ran down the road and saw the man lying face down. I called on my mobile 999, got the police and shouted for assistance - then went to the man expecting him to be dead, yet all the time saying 'Let him live God'. As I turned him over he opened his eyes, and said, "*Thank God I am alive, I need the toilet!*" He got up and rushed over the bank and dropped his trousers. Nobody was injured and I just put out my arms and thanked God.

What we think and say from our consciousness magnetises everything to us. Even in a crisis what is in our soul and heart can serve and protect us. The more we go within to that abundant, trusting, loving place the more our lives will turn towards a light within, a light that reveals such grace, where miracles are natural not abnormal. Learn to expect miracles, they are not just coincidences, if you think and say and act with deep loving intentions, the miracles of love, healing, creativity, happiness and abundance will come back multiplied.

VISUALISE
Right now visualise love pouring out from the top of your head into the room, the country, the world you are in. Let whatever visions come to you, and say or run through your mind: "*I am connected to an unlimited divine abundance of love.*" Then say it and repeat it as you walk or sit and just notice the miracle of living life unfold. And so it is.

FEELING WORTHY OF LOVE
Often I sit and hear a person say. "*Well I am not worth anything, my life is a failure and I would be better off dead*". Sometimes the phone will ring and a far off voice will say, "*I can't go on any longer, I am off the planet, help me, ground me I need to have some hope*". Memories of deep childhood abuse can ruin a life. The feeling of shame and guilt can resurface at a moment's notice. It can be like living with a gun to your head, which has a hair

trigger. A word, a smell, a place, a program on TV, and a partner wanting sex in a particular way can pull the trigger. You feel unworthy of being alive. Thinking the worst in any situation can produce just that. To be around a male with certain hair can trigger an abnormal pulse and a wish to flee. It can be such a lonely place even in a room with people if you're back in a memory. Having said this, I could write a book about abuse, however I want to give real hope that you can learn to think and feel worthy, to live life and give your unique love to loving yourself and others. As you think and believe you are a miracle worthy of love, you will attract exactly that.

"The essential sadness is to go through life not loving. But it would be almost equally sad to leave this world without ever telling those you loved, that you loved them".
John Powell one writer in "Chicken soup for the soul"

If I ask a person to say the simple affirmation, and remember every thought is an affirmation, *"I love and approve of myself"*, so often it's like watching a person saying the unthinkable, because they can never remember being told they were loved. It's like seeing a crumpled child in a grown body. Learning to choose thoughts and feelings that give healing life back into our hearts and soul is not easy for the abused yet it can and is possible, you and I have a choice to deserve love from ourselves to all parts of us or we stay hoping somebody will love us. People, who come from unloving backgrounds, are not taught at school how our human mind works and how to use the mind in such a way that true healing can take place. So whatever went on in the past can be brought to the present, yet not swamp the present life you are living.

When you have been abused your body mind and spirit do not think and feel like a miracle. You can easily choose thoughts that hurt you, re-abuse you or others and you think you can't stop. Sometimes people come for counseling and are not ready to go within and learn that they are lovable. They return later when old lessons that have not been learnt, keep re-occurring, until somebody gives them time, space, love and new knowledge. Awareness without understanding new knowledge, inner wisdom and learning to love who we really are can keep us stuck in the past as though it's the present. There are some people walking the planet like this at present, stuck in the past with no new inner knowledge to live their life differently. Many of these adults are hurt children who "grow up" and can create corrupt governments, some with torture and abuse. Where inner poverty reigns, poor thinking and feeling patterns can create rigid beliefs; this can permeate the culture of a relationship, family, housing estate, work place and government. The choice can appear to be either you join "them," carrying on hating and hurting yourself and more likely to abuse others, or you allow a deep intuitive knowing inside you to reveal other more loving ways to live your life. Here are a few hard won guidelines that I have found helpful to choose life. You may disagree, yet if you find one that helps, great! So often in my learning, my inner child has rebelled (from a scolding parent) and not wanted to learn anything, much later I realized what was being suggested would be helpful. For a long time I wanted to lead with my wounds, it was my only protection and identity, not healthy! I forgive me now.

FEELING WORTHY

1. Understand your mind can heal you if you choose loving and gentle thoughts. Which are you going to keep choosing? Thoughts that hurt and criticize you or thoughts that forgive and love you and those around you. The power that is there for you, I believe is a loving and healing presence. We learn to have our own unique relationship with the power that made us, not an institutionalized one that is imposed by people who don't love the miracle they are. So often the wounded blind lead the wounded blind, learn to think in your unique mind!

2. Do you realize you choose the thoughts in your mind, not your mind choosing them for you? You have ultimate control nobody can think in your mind. A woman has just telephoned saying she is "trapped by the church, her friends, her husband, and having no job..." This may seem how it is, yet if this wonderful powerful woman started to choose to stop blaming and be gentle on herself and start seeing how she is making herself wrong, her experience will change. By the end of the conversation she saw what she was doing, and began to see the family pattern of making herself feel wrong. She learnt this pattern from a mother who rejected anything she did; now she was carrying on the same pattern. She congratulated herself by the end of the conversation, and realized she can think in her mind and let go of what other people may or may not be thinking about her.

3. You have a higher mind and lower mind. The lower mind will often feed you old negative tapes learnt in childhood. John Bradshaw estimates we have twenty five thousand hours of childhood tapes, often negative. These tapes are stored in our subconscious mind. We have to consciously make the higher mind work for us, go past the pain and memories (without denial) and feed in new files of positive tapes with lots of positive messages. (My inner

child wants to play with the size of the words as I type this. He has just informed me he'd like to go for a bike ride with the dog. My inner parent says get serious! Now we're co-operating, we will go for a walk.) You won't understand this if you have not read chapter 6!

4. Day by day learn to write and say positive affirmations, just accept the gift from your higher mind and when you do it into a mirror, which is powerful. Thank yourself for being so bright and clever. Remember *OUR WORDS CREATE OUR REALITY*.

5. Learn to dialogue with your inner child each day. This will show you where your inner conversations often stop you being and doing what you want. This will regenerate the genius of your inner child that is at one with being a miracle.

6. Learn, read and listen to tapes that are from people who are positive role models and come from a loving intention, who are learning to love who they are, this will cultivate our higher mind. So many of us who have been abused or just feel unworthy, are starved of good information. Mean business; stop the TV and watching negative films and news, spend time being creative. This may sound prescriptive or idealistic, yet it is so easy to think life is hopeless and soak up the TV and then say, *"I'll never change and grow"*. Yes you can if you make a conscious decision; the point of power is now.

Please hear this, I am not saying deny your past, you may need to go on anger workshops, re-claiming your inner child; be in touch with your feelings and emotions. And eventually you will need to move on, not stay stuck in the past and choose to live in the present. You have probably been angry far too long.

7. Have fun leaning to love you, lighten up. Dance down the street, my kids leave me then! See how many people pass you in the street and send them love and radiate a smile. Sing in the bath, jump in the puddles, draw, paint and create in everything you do and congratulate you for 'getting it'. When you email or write think loving, joyful, healing, and compassionate and prosperity thoughts. Then just see what the universe returns.

8. "No man is an island" John Dunne. Learn to meditate and pray. I do yoga and I love to meditate afterwards. Keep it simple I have put a few suggestions in the book. Read, "Manifest your Destiny" by Dr Wayne Dyer and "Minding the Body, Mending the Mind", by Dr Joan Borysenko and her latest book Inner Peace for Busy People. She explains in very simple ways how to replace stress with a deep inner peace that helps you think and act positively in your life.

9. Look after your body. As you make a decision to choose thoughts that forgive and love you, let your higher self, guide you to learn about your body, what food and exercise feed your soul and body.

Right now you may be having inner conversations, I haven't got time I work too hard, well love them enough to let them go and choose to turn each critical thought time into a positive affirmation. How long have you argued for your limitations? Say out loud,

"IT IS SAFE TO CHANGE AND GROW,
I LOVE TO LEARN AND LIVE MY LIFE NOW!"

WHEN YOUR READY TELL US YOUR STORY
I have typed this chapter with a passion of a child that wants so much to feel people can learn to love who they are and create an inner peace, I cannot do it for you. Whatever age, country, race, religion or no religion you have been brought up in, I would love you to tell your story of how you have learnt to love the miracle you are. Something about what has inspired the divine spark in you. This I believe will touch others and your story will spark other individual miracles to write their healing story and this can send love into every corner of this planet, in ways we cannot yet imagine. Yet what's the choice stay the same or take a DIVINE RISK? Take the DIVINE RISK TO LOVE YOU AND MANIFEST THE MIRACLE IN YOU. Whether you are a child, teenager, so called adult like me, who has never written anything before, just pass this heart affirmation through your mind.

"With divine love inside of me now, I am able to write about what has made me as I am and what has healed me. The ideas and thoughts come easily and lovingly and my spark of love helps others to do the same around the world."

As I write this, I listen to my children talking from their bedrooms, one is reading the other is playing his story tapes to relax himself as he goes to sleep. Both express such a natural love and trust for life. I give thanks for all my children. As I go to sleep I ask my higher self to guide and protect me during my sleep. I give over any problem I have to that special loving universe, the loving thoughtful God that made me. And so it is.

EXERCISE
What is your family pattern of thinking that can make you think and feel wrong?

MEDITATION

FEELINGS

As I safely learn to express difficult feelings.
I realise I am not those feelings.

Yet they help me release the past that holds me stuck.
Feelings are thoughts running through my body.

Loving thoughts create loving feelings that heal
every organ and cell in my body.
And so it is.

CHAPTER 8
We Can Change the World by Each Changing Ourselves

"When I loved myself enough I quit trying to be a saviour for others."
Kim & Alison McMillen

How do you start your day? I used to get up complaining and I fall back to this way of thinking when I forget what a treasure life is, inside and around me. I used to shout or not talk at all. I learnt I could frighten people by my moods. Not clever ways of creating my life, making others tiptoe around me. The problem was it made me attract the same moodiness in the people I chose to be in relationship with and certainly in the clients I counseled. This is not a judgment it is a fact, as I radiated moods of anger and criticism, I attracted that in my daily life from others.

The idea that if I changed my inner world and how I related to that small world of family, work and community, that I could make a difference, sounded ungrounded and brain washing in my limited thinking. You may have similar patterns of thinking, "just look after No1". However we are all joined on a soul level, what I think, say and do in my life connects to your life somewhere. If we are all unhappy and poor in our thinking, we then spread these negative thoughts like locusts, what kind of world are we creating?

No matter how devout our beliefs and prayers, how well read we are, clever or rich we are, if our day starts with yells, screams and moods we spread our unhappiness onto others. This means we are adding to the conscious message that we are not worthy of touching the treasure of life and love within and around us on a daily basis. This can and is changing when we connect to the treasure of a universal love deep at the centre of our being.

THOUGHTS CREATE, SO LOVING THOUGHTS CREATE MORE LOVING THOUGHTS

People living a truth, that our thoughts are creative have chosen to know there is a deep infinite well of love, joy, peace and wisdom at their core. By learning to love us a little more each day, this radiates healing love to every person and experience we meet. Even when we make mistakes we learn from them instead of repeating them.

No matter how cynical you are or fearful of letting go of your hate or guilt, just think how precious your breath is right now. Would you want somebody to stop you breathing? I hope the answer is "no." You would fight hard to keep breathing. Well imagine there is in each breath a love you could breath in and out of your mind, only instead of air it's what you choose to think and create. Right now you could say something negative or you could choose:

"I am filled with unconditional love and I express it now."

"I am filled with joy and peace and I express it now."

"I am filled with abundant wisdom and I practice it today in my life and this is the real miracle in me."

Today, a woman rang saying, *"I like what I do but I hate the environment I work in"*. We have worked together for a year, and I just replied *"What positive thought could you write to yourself right now?"* She replied *"respect, good boss, love my work, an increasing income and friendly co-workers, plus in exactly the right location"*. She rang me back and with a different energy and voice relaying this affirmation.

"I bless the job I have with love and let it go to exactly the right person, who will do an excellent job. And I now easily attract the right job and loving people, increasing my income for my skills and talents. It's in the right area and I enjoy the work, and I am really grateful."

Now you could say, "who's kidding who?" A year ago she did not have the information and I would be kidding her, yet now she has proved to herself, repeatedly she can create through her thoughts what she wants, by coming to herself from deep respect for who she is and knowing she deserves the best! So knowing this woman well she means business. I salute her faith and hard work to change her whole life, from being a victim and persecutor, really angry and fearful, to a woman who takes responsibility for her life and has STOPPED BLAMING herself and the world! When she first came, I asked her to say each morning into the mirror, "I love and approve of you". This was agony for her, she was planting a seed in a garden of consciousness that had many weeds of fear and rocks of criticism, and now with time and persistent repetition she believes this affirmation. Jerry Frankhauser describes "Affirmations are like prescriptions for certain aspects of yourself that you want to change." Who do you think can help change this world for the better, the woman who hated herself or the one who is learning to love the miracle power inside her? People say you teach people to be selfish and it's too simplistic, well if learning to love you and the power that made us, which I assume is love, is wrong I stand accused! Yet I know I would rather be around people who take back the power of love and radiate this to life, than create hate and fear, criticism and guilt. I know each of us has pain, yet we have a choice to use that pain to grow rather than keep creating more pain. Remember what you are choosing to think now will create your future experiences.

MAKE THE TRANSITION FROM ANGER TO LOVING

Sometimes if we have never said what we feel or think, because of our past programming, it can seem such a leap to be real and not get rejected. Today I have had some tough sessions, with people who fear 'if I am real in what I say and feel, I'll hurt or be hurt and nobody will love me'. This cycle can seem unending, yet this pattern learnt in childhood can be worked through with easy steps.

Anger bottled up for years pollutes. Once owned, then released safely and let go, will distil the taste for revenge. This moves onto dissolving resistance and believing and feeling you deserve good in your life. When you feel emotional distance from your own self, partner and those close to you, it's so hard, or you are single and feel so lonely. The idea that saying and writing positive present affirmations seems so paradoxically opposite to your reality. IT IS! At first when some bright person said, "Say a positive thought into a mirror and write them down", I thought they did live on a different planet and I was being in denial of my process. Then they added "and do it hundreds of times in a day", I thought, "You must be joking". All my counselling training and beliefs were being challenged. My resistance was anger, ridicule and total disbelief. Then I caught my thoughts of such ferocious resistance and these questions came into my mind. Why do I like to keep hold of my misery? Why do I want to attract to me more pain? Do I perversely like pain for the sake of it? Then there was fear, real fear. If I let go of so-called negative thoughts and feelings, what would be left of me? Then the thought came, *"What if I dared experiment with changing the thoughts in my mind?"* The idea somebody may be a bit further along the pathway of loving and living life to the full triggered my computer brain into questioning everything. This included how I had used my past and my reactions to it, to give myself meaning even if I had chosen it, to survive the best way I knew how, it was not supporting my life. I kept repeating the same mistakes; the same experience kept on being repeated, with variations on a theme. I was beginning to confront me! I didn't like it yet I knew somewhere I had to do it, if I was going to find me, live with me and eventually love living life.

As I write this I am strangely excited, because so many people have learnt to argue vehemently for their limitations. Yet I did not see my resistance to loving me. I thought I was honoring my process, I had got so used to beating myself up and listening to others do the same. I really believed this was my purpose to help other people have their pain and their process, and they would eventually change and heal. Yet if I couldn't move on and heal, forgive, love and create, how could I truly be there for others who wanted to change?

My energy was being sucked out of my soul, with me arguing against myself. And boy have I got clever resistance that has kept me going in that circle of "being right" even if it killed me! Somehow I thought "I CAN MAKE MYSELF RIGHT BY THINKING AND FEELING WRONG." The fact that I needed an abundance of love and forgiveness by choosing to change my thoughts and attracting to myself experiences which reflected my new thinking was too simple for the complex coping strategy for living, which I had built over many years. So a vital precarious step is to watch the clever, or not so clever thoughts you feed yourself in not deserving love. We can put so much energy into negative thoughts. When I started writing and saying positive affirmations, especially into a mirror, the inner embarrassment was making my inner conversations go wild. I was also shut down to the higher wisdom of divine understanding and intuition. So one of my affirmations that I am writing and saying is:

"I am letting divine intelligence express through me now. I am worthy of love and this changes my experiences. I have unlimited vision for seeing and experiencing good. I am open and receptive to my highest good in the form of new understanding, new experiences, and I give thanks."

RECEIVING PROSPERITY

Say out loud wherever you are now; if you would embarrass yourself pass it through your mind with your arms wide open.

"I am open and receptive to prosperity of all kinds."

What comes up for you? Just before I went to sleep last night, I asked the universal mind to reveal the next chapter. I awoke this morning at 3.30am feeling my inner conversations going wild. In my childhood money always seemed scarce. I learned to be frightened around my parents when they talked about a continual lack of money. When money was mentioned in my family the association was lack of love and trust. I can recall now my father throwing money at my mother telling her to buy us shoes, while she accused him of spending it on his women. This negative family pattern has formed thoughts like: "Money will bring unhappiness." The consequence of this was the thought "Just get by, others can earn money but I must not."

FALSE BELIEFS

This is not a healthy inner conversation, it has made me choose an erroneous belief; "I will not go to heaven if I am rich." At church as a young choirboy I can remember sermons of the rich being dammed and saying inside I must give money away if I ever had any.

One thought that you may identify with is never being good enough or clever enough to earn good money; this can be reinforced in the classroom and in certain religions. This is not healthy thinking; prosperity equals money, which I must not have and I don't deserve. It also links the word prosperity to just money. Listening to tapes on "Receiving Prosperity" and reading a book called "Creating Money Keys to Abundance" by Sanaya Roman & Duane Packer, I am beginning to shift my consciousness. That as I love the miracle I am, it is OK to earn money in a totally different conscious way than what was taught me, when young.

As I come to myself and others from, a higher consciousness, my soul, the deepest part of my being, or the God power within me, then what I create, will be for the benefit of all, including me. I deserve to express and create from a totally different level of consciousness. Run this affirmation through your mind:

"I deserve to come from abundance, and I am at one with the source that creates abundance.
I am an open channel for wealth of every kind to flow through me now."

WHAT IS PROSPERITY?

I am learning we can be prosperous in time, health, job, comfort, spirit, love, trust, wisdom, awareness, success, relationships, happiness and money. Prosperity is not exclusive to money. People can be happy with little money, so money is not the answer yet it is often the easiest form to manifest when you or I really love who we are. "Money has no intrinsic value, it is only a means of exchange", Louise Hay. We can be prosperous with money but poor in time always racing from one situation to the next. We may have little trust, I certainly wasn't prosperous in trust and a few of the others mentioned above. As you invest positive thoughts in the "cosmic bank account" of your consciousness you will attract to you such abundance, everyday when I go for a walk I open my arms wide and say *"I am open and receptive to..."* whatever I feel in need of and the universe provides!

FOLLOWING SIMPLE SPIRITUAL LAWS

I am challenging an old negative and self-defeating belief in my subconscious mind. One of these was to seek permission from others about being successful and letting their values limit me. I have always told myself from past mistakes, "I am not business minded" and "I will lose money rather than make any." Find what you love to do and do it with love. Do what makes your heart sing and have a skip in your stride! God does not have poverty consciousness, money is not evil, and it can be used for good or wrong like anything else. I am beginning to see and think more clearly that many of us have not learnt what Sanaya & Duane say "follow spiritual laws of money when you do your life's work and honour and serve the higher good of others. You follow the spiritual laws when you cooperate rather than compete with others, making every energy and money exchange a winning situation for everyone involved. You follow the spiritual laws of money when the way you make, spend, or invest money does not harm the earth." Then add, "Money will be a by-product of doing what you love and will flow effortlessly into your life, without even much thought."

Your thoughts create the perfect job. Often people will say, "I hate my job and I have to do it because I have to survive!" I ask them "Have you ever put thoughts into your mind like the following?"

"I bless my present job with love and I release this job to a person
who is perfect and does a great job."

Then add:

> *"Divine guidance is attracting the right job that I love doing,
> with people who respect me, the work uses my creative talents with abundant
> prosperity in all areas of my life and in a wonderful location and I
> go to work with joy and I give thanks! "*

Remember if I only say this twice a day, which is great, what if my thoughts for the rest of the day are negative; I will not let go the old limiting beliefs and move on. Please hear me I am not denying your reality of feeling trapped in a job, yet if you keep saying what you don't want; how can anything good come into your experience of life except your old limiting beliefs? Change what you choose to think, and say, your experience will then change for the positive.

PLANT GOOD SEEDS

Self-approval without guilt, you accepting you just as you are, will open the gate to a garden that you have so often refused to enter. This garden is full of simple lessons with clear directions, if you follow them, you will start creating and planting your unique seeds, these seeds are thoughts of love, forgiveness, healing, play, creativity, happiness and relationships that prosper you and this earth. Going within gently, thinking peacefully, past all the pain and your history, will I believe help open this gate. Our senses will reveal energy of thought and experience, with patience, all our old coping strategies of cynicism will gradually dissolve. In this garden we learn to clear the old beliefs, fears, anger and guilt gently. Then in our unique way we start finding new thought seeds that "bubble up inside us", asking us to think them, say them and plant them with each breath. Think clearly and quietly what you want. This will come, the more positive thoughts and emotions you have, the more you will be open to the divine intention and allow what you truly want to come into your mind. Your inner child will give you gifts of intelligence and creativity you never knew you had, make sure your inner parent encourages your child and the prosperity of awareness, knowledge and wisdom will build a new level of consciousness.

Our mind has the capacity to learn deep truths, when our inner child, the miracle we are, is free from a scolding parent. As you start saying any statement with DIVINE LOVE you will engage an energy that creates beyond our imagination. Right now I am focusing on starting a publishing company. The name is 'Soul Talk Stories' with a website www.soultalkstories.com. Note: A year ago I wrote the above and the affirmation below, now in December 2003 it is a reality. I just give thanks. The heart affirmation I wrote a week ago is this:

Divine love is manifesting people to write and send their healing
stories about "Learning to love and live the miracle they are."
This sparks the miracle of love in those who read these stories and they
freely choose to write and send their positive
stories to www.soultalkstories.com.
We create and send love around the planet across all
barriers and this helps to heal the planet.

Two days later I received the first story called "Learning to Love Yourself: The Never-Ending Story", it is wonderful. Now 28 stories are on the website.

LISTEN AND TRUST YOUR INTUITION

I have just left a man, who had tried to commit suicide. As I met him, I had a strong intuitive message to ask him to consider writing his story. Before I asked him he was remembering that at the age of 18, he told a teacher he wanted to be a writer. He was informed, "That's not a profession", and so he never took it up. He now has written his story which will be published on the Soul Talk Story website. Another young man has dropped his moving story into my lap, and shown me how to copy it onto my computer!

Ask yourself. *"What have I always wanted to be and do in my life?"* Then go within and listen. Something may just bubble up, listen and trust it may come up sometime later.

WHAT IS YOUR VISION?

Do you stand in front of a sea of abundance with "a hole in my bucket dear Liza?" Or do you have a pipeline consciousness that is willing to:

- Magnetise to you what you want.
- Let go of old beliefs.
- Learn and follow spiritual laws of creating prosperity.
- Create your real talents and the work you love.
- Listen to your higher self and manifest your destiny.
- Choose thoughts that free your "wonder child" with a nurturing parent.

Simple Steps, that will help achieve the above

1. Stop criticizing yourself about wanting to earn a good income.

2. Realize money is not the answer, yet it is part of our divine birthright to be prosperous in all areas of our life.

3. Learning to love you, and using our minds well, will create abundance.

4. Keep doing the mirror affirmation work. Your eyes in the mirror will always tell you deep messages of resistance. Write them down and create clear positive affirmations. Remember to thank the resistant old thoughts for sharing, and then move onto the positive affirmations. Make a song out of your affirmations, repeat, repeat and repeat.

5. Do the inner conversations between your inner child and parent. Here your love between your inner parent and child will grow and this will translate positively into your present life.

6. Create clear simple thoughts that become your new beliefs that truly support your vision. When you think I will take a year to start that project, support yourself and bring the project forward to say 3 months. The universe will support you.

7. Don't let those around you convince you that you are wrong to want abundance in your life you deserve abundance. Be patient and enjoy working on yourself and your mind. Each time you're jealous of others who are successful realize you have some work to do.

8. Read books, listen to tapes; "Receiving Prosperity" by Louise Hay is an excellent tape.

9. Do it NOW - don't wait - enjoy learning about creating abundance in your life.

SOME AFFIRMATIONS:

"I ALWAYS DO WORK I LOVE."

"I ATTRACT PEOPLE WHO ARE EASY TO WORK WITH AND WE HAVE FUN BEING CREATIVE."

"MY INCOME IS CONTINUALLY INCREASING."

"I AM ALWAYS OPEN AND RECEPTIVE TO ABUNDANCE IN EVERY AREA OF MY LIFE."

"I LET GO OF OLD LIMITING BELIEFS OF OTHERS AND MYSELF."

"I CHOOSE FRIENDS WHO SUPPORT ME IN MY GROWTH."

"THE RIGHT WORK COMES AT THE RIGHT TIME."

"I SPEND MONEY WISELY."

"I GIVE 100 PERCENT IN ALL THAT I DO AND
I DO IT TO THE BEST OF MY ABILITY."

EXERCISE

• What comes up when you say, "My biggest fear about money is..." What are your first thoughts? I viewed those who create wealth as bad, so if I earned money and I was successful others wouldn't like me.

• What are your negative belief patterns?

• WHAT WERE YOUR PARENTS BELIEFS ABOUT MONEY? Nobody taught me about the spiritual laws of prosperity, yet self worth was tied to money in many subtle ways "work hard and you'll get on, get your grades, go to college and get a good job". The only bit that was missing was me, I had no idea of who I was or what I loved doing. People often have more negative triggers on money than sex or health. Whenever money is mentioned it's like something has crawled out of the carpet and is bad!

MEDITATION

PURPOSE

As we connect to the power within.
Our souls join in harmony.
And so it is.

CHAPTER 9
Empowerment

"Men can love themselves in ways that children and women love."
My inner child

*"I look forward to this day with eagerness, excitement and know
that this day will be the best day of my life."*
My inner parent

What does that bring up for you on a cold winter morning? The baby may
be screaming, your husband's at work, or you're single, unemployed, perhaps
divorced, doing a job you hate, and the list of things to do is growing. All
you feel is that something inside is going mad, and you go from one negative
situation to the other. Sex is a chore, the partner (if we have one) doesn't listen
to us, and 'just functioning' is the order of the day. Money is short, the bills
are huge and parenting your children is hard work. So many of us can choose
to live like this, we survive in a functioning fog, where we just learn to react
like a ball in a pinball machine. We feel out of control, someone else pulls
the plunger and we just bounce from one situation to the next, stacking up
a really heavy negative score, with our thoughts and feelings just racing
round. Then something wakes you up, a kick in the soul.

THE INNER WAKE UP CALL
When I thought the world would be better off without me, when all my past
invaded me and I became victim to it. I remembered my Buddhist teacher
Ole Larsen saying. "Do you want to change and grow Roger? Do you

want to take responsibility for your life?" The answer was inside my head "You don't understand." I was an angry inner child; I wanted others to rescue me, then he confronted me with "you make such a drama out of your life, start living now." The language of growth, love, happiness, personal power, abundance, forgiveness, and thinking clearly, dissolving barriers to loving yourself, creating a job you enjoy, attracting and building a great relationship and learning to be a parent-this was a foreign language to me. The person who lived in my world just had poor relationships and little self-awareness, as old thought patterns and past hurts were being played out like old tapes. Having been there, I am amazed and marvel when a person chooses from this suicidal place to learn: HOW TO LOVE THEMSELVES! The old life of re-abuse, rejection, bitterness, depression, and addiction to blame does not blot out the pulse of love that is there for you and me. If we are willing to do one thing, STOP ALL CRITICISM NOW AND IN THE FUTURE. When you and I make ourselves wrong it immediately puts us back into the role of victim. Wherever you are now, whatever you are doing, make an agreement to STOP BLAMING. I always wanted other people to change then I would change, I was always innocent, I didn't want to know I had control. The first thing I had to admit was that I made my life suicidal by blaming. Learning to be responsible for me completely changed my way of thinking and behaving.

Imagine living in a country where you can't speak the language, you feel so powerless to make yourself and others understand you. Well this book is like a simple dictionary and map, to guide you on the first steps to loving you and treating you with deep respect. Remember when I say, "*learning to love you*" I don't mean love that comes from fear or guilt, that comes from the ego, an acronym, for "Earth Guide Only since ego represents our exclusive identification with our physical selves in our material world." Dr Wayne Dyer. It's about a deep respect for the MIRACLE that you are, and consequently how you treat yourself, your children and partner and friends. You can see yourself as depressed, a drug addict, co-dependant, labeled by professionals, and that is what you can create for the rest of your life. I met a large woman in a group, who as I talked about HOW TO LOVE ourselves, blurted out that she had hit her disabled son 18 months ago and could not forgive herself. So she decided to eat and eat to punish herself. As the whole group gave her such compassion she realized how she was punishing herself. It was wonderful seeing the relief in her soul as she could stop blaming herself and begin to see what she was doing. I had seen this lady two days before at a concert being carried out on a stretcher with a suspected heart attack. I thought then, 'I wonder if our paths will cross.' The universe moved fast. You may label yourself a Muslim, Christian, Hindu, Buddhist, Jewish, Socialist, agnostic, atheist, humanist whoever, whatever, yet you all have the capacity to choose thoughts in your mind to "love the miracle that you are". And as you learn this, you will create a life, that lets go the past, however bad that past is. Then become fully present to being the authentic YOU, with all the different selves that make you special.

LOVING YOURSELF IS NOT A SIN

Learning to love from a place of deep self-respect and self-acceptance only good wells up from within you. The resistance will be there, like "You must be joking", just thank those negative thoughts for sharing, and choose thoughts and words that are life enhancing. Like "I am good enough just as I am." with "I am learning and it's OK to make mistakes." Now, no matter what your outer circumstances are, just keep going within to that experience of being a miracle. For a whole day just build a wonderful experience inside you of you as a baby inside your heart, carry that baby which is you and talk to yourself beautiful loving thoughts and begin to re-parent you.

Imagine you carrying and holding the new born you, what would you give that baby and say to that baby. Sit in front of a mirror and just say how much you love the baby inside. Even witness people with babies, really look at that baby, without being intrusive, I love to see babies, perhaps it's just that there is no judgement, it's amazing how people become magnetised to new born babies. Just for the next week take your baby in your heart, make it that size and love him or her, then gradually grow that baby.

GIVE YOURSELF PERMISSION

When I met my second partner, we would spend so much time being babies. Sometimes we would compete for time to be a baby. It's so healing to let you be a baby. Often when I am windsurfing I see grown men and women yelling with delight at the pleasures of being free to yell and shout their joy. Babies and children love to scream with delight. Do it, some anger and sadness may come, and then a new fountain of love will come as you keep saying "I DESERVE LOVE FOR JUST BEING ME, A MIRACLE." What you are building is self-worth, while it may sound too simple for you who want complex explanations; the fact is you are worthy because you say so.

EMPOWERING MEN TO LOVE

Learning to love the child within and parenting can become a pleasure not a nightmare. Rob Parsons in his book "Sixty Minute Father" is a poignant reminder to men, in particular who put work, telephones or anything else before being a parent. In one survey, men were asked "How long do you think you spend each day in conversations with your toddler?" Most men guessed at between fifteen and twenty minutes a day. To test this, the researchers put microphones on the father and the children to measure accurately the amount of parental interaction. Those busy men spent on average less than forty seconds a day with their children, split into three encounters of between ten and fifteen seconds each. In another survey the fathers were spending 3 minutes a day talking with their children but the research showed that the children were watching three hours of television a day.

All human beings are unique we cannot be categorised. Yet this small survey shows how parenting, especially for men, is still such a difficult, unknown territory. If young boys have not been loved, talked to, listened to and played with consistently and with quality how can they learn to be loving, caring and playful fathers and understand the emotional intelligence for a successful relationship. This is a challenge for empowering men to want to learn parenting, by re-parenting their own lost and forgotten child. So many of my female clients, who have children, often say, "if only my husband or partner could listen and play with the children". 'What do you really want for your children?' By Dr Wayne Dyer is an excellent book to read about creating a climate of self-worth where children can grow in valuing themselves, becoming self-reliant risk-takers, and have the inner resources to fulfil their potential. Parenting becomes an exciting and mutually satisfying adventure of learning and creating for all involved.

EMOTIONAL INTIMACY

So many men ask me, "How do I get close to my partner or my daughter?" I suggest they ask them and listen with full attention and on all levels. I have just left a man whose anger and grief still lingers from splitting up from his wife. Men I ask you to find and love all the lost ages of the child within you. We want so much love and approval yet think we are so strong, we are not from Mars, we can be emotionally and intelligently present for our intimate relationships and ourselves. Go for it men love to change how you communicate within and risk letting the tears come from the lack of love and approval you got as a child. Love that child and your whole emotional intelligence will change.

Here are some affirmations for men who want to balance their masculine and female energies.

"I am discovering how sensitive and playful I am."

"I see a playful child that loves to play and create."

"I am a caring listener to my partner, children and friends."

"I use my inner-directed power wisely and with love."

"I admit when I make mistakes."

"I make choices in my life."

"I am learning that blame reinforces bad thoughts and feelings."

"I am open to new ways of relating to my partner and children."

"I am willing to learn how to be a passionate and a sensitive lover."

"When there is work to be done around the house I enjoy doing it."

"I am worthy of love."

"I enjoy both my masculine and feminine capabilities."

"I don't beat myself up when I make mistakes."

MAKE YOUR OWN
What you believe and talk becomes true for you. As you take responsibility for your own life, everything outside will change and grow towards the positive. Yes you may slip back, you may just see problems, only this time laugh and don't beat yourself up! Then create thoughts like:

"I give myself permission to learn how to use my mind in new, positive and loving ways. I don't beat myself up when I make mistakes. I re-learn how to become a powerful loving person, with a well of love so abundant inside of me. I let go of the past and live in the present and I re-parent myself, building true self-worth. And I have fun learning. And so it is."

TIME AND PATIENCE
Sometimes, positive writers and speakers can appear light years away for 'us mortals', who think, "well I couldn't do what she's done or he's done".

That may be true YOU CAN ONLY BE YOURSELF. Yet there are truths of how we use our mind, body and spirit that can release us from the bondage of being a victim, a persecutor and wanting to be rescued all the time. In my personal experiences and in counseling others, no matter how bad the story is, if you choose deep down to change and grow - you will read, listen and learn and translate positive thoughts into reality.

"As I learn to go within I am willing to change and grow.
I discover new insights into making my reality positive and
inner-directed. This creates a self-worth of real inner love and fun.
I love to read and learn from people who love who they are, my relationships hum
with new vitality.
I love life and all life supports me."

EXERCISE
Just go within and imagine yourself as a newborn baby, totally loving you, with no fears, no guilt, and no criticism you are an expression of love, trusting and accepting. There is no prejudice in your mind; you have been so close to the universal mind that made you.

As you go within, see and experience your baby within, what happens? Go deep and just feel, see and act as a baby, what kind of thoughts and feelings do you have? Perhaps you can feel, touch and sense the thoughts and feelings of your baby inside. Cuddle yourself under a duvet. Just watch what comes up and let the feelings flow.

Part IV
Moving On

CHAPTER 10
Giving Thanks for Being Heard by Someone Special

This morning I awoke to share the pain and love I have with my partner Linda. We talked and listened to each other for hours. We often do this; it keeps us both on track for knowing what is going on inside. I give a deep thank you for my partner's willingness to share her deepest inner thoughts and feelings, her inner conversations. We realize this process of deep listening is so healing; it's like touching the love of God deep inside another "human" being. When I separate from my partner by choosing thoughts of me being wrong or her being wrong and we make our love conditional, it hurts me deep inside, and I know it hurts her. When I appear to make her wrong and myself right or vice versa, our love is on pause. When we really listen and give thanks to each other for risking deep pain, then the drops of pain slowly come out and love starts to rise with the internal pain healed. For years I have been healed by being listened to, and listening to Linda. It's like a healing love that goes deep into my soul.

The process of deep sharing is like a wind that blows away the fog of thoughts and feelings, which can easily become deeply critical and angry. If I stay on pause by justifying my position and I am unwilling to listen or share, so much of my pain is recycled and I keep beating others or myself up in my mind. I certainly don't give thanks for life and all the blessings around me. I just judge and this sets me up to become ungrateful. Then it's as though I put on the radio, listen to the negative news and get fuel for my critical judgmental thoughts, or start gossip in my mind. My fears grow and I just go round in an ever-decreasing circle of hopelessness.

BEING HEARD

To break this cycle of being critical and resentful, of anger taken in on myself, I need to be heard by someone I know who loves me just for who I am. Sometimes I can do this for myself by sitting meditating with the God of love within, yet other times I need my partner Linda to touch me gently and lovingly then it's as though my inner child comes alive. When I will not give thanks for my relationships, what I have, who I am, the gift of life, the air I breathe, and I want more and more materially, I know this is a sign for going within and speaking and listening from a deep place. Pain often comes, tears and emotions, yet also what comes is a peace, creativity or knowing a wonder child that wants to play and have fun and most of all GIVE THANKS. I become more in tune with my body, mind and soul.

This rich vein of sharing with another person is, I am sure, what each of us needs at various times in our lives. As a counselor, I come with the intention to give deep attention to the person. Sometimes I am fully present but I do make mistakes. I love experiencing the growth by sharing their life and the truth of their pain, and then love can mix with that pain and turn a person's life to seeing what a miracle they truly are. Yesterday a woman came up to me and said "I think the penny has dropped I am learning to love all of me. I have just got my son out of care and this time I am learning to play and listen to him. I see if I love me and take my power back I can learn how to re-love my son, even when he gets angry with me."

I pray that each of you reading this can learn to create in you the qualities you want in your partner and so attract that special person in your life that you can share with and listen to. It's like going within and holding hands together to meet with a God of love and an infinite mind that helps us. Keep giving thanks and the heavens will open. You will have so much more to be thankful for. YOU DESERVE LOVE SO YOU CAN LOVE WITH COMPASSION AND MAKE HEALING YOUR BUSINESS.

SEX OR MAKING LOVE?

The act of making physical love as you accept all the different parts of you, warts and all, is such a different experience to when you just have sex. Often I hear, "I want to be held. I want to know we are in tune with each other. I can't have orgasms.... ". Bernie Seigel's book "Love Medicine and Miracles" talks about intimate caring love for those without limbs due to cancer. Making love can just be holding each other, and giving love with such heart love. We can dissolve old stereotypes of lovemaking. When I did not like me, I could have sex and found I hated myself rather than enjoy the experience. One real transformation in my life is making love and being in the present, and making love from my soul, the heart of my being. Then the act of love is a unique experience with the same partner who loves me.

When I first started to look into a mirror I hated what I saw, I always mistrusted myself mentally and sexually. I could not look myself in my own eyes and say, "I love you just as you are". All I could say was "you're rotten", I had taken in beliefs about my body that mirrored the partners I attracted. Sex was a physical release and became a near addiction because I could not love myself. I became so critical of my own body including my genitals, sex became painful mentally, emotionally and physically, and there was no spiritual contact except feeling "I am damned". This gradually changed as I confronted myself with one huge opposite thought; "I love you just as you are." I was repeatedly and consistently telling myself that there is a natural lovely soul inside of me, not just a soul that is BAD, WRONG, DISGUSTING and that's evil. Those thoughts did not serve me-they made me worse. So if you find yourself in an ever tightening thought and feeling loop, which condemns you, for whatever reason, (you may have been abused, rejected, whatever - I do not minimise your past or present). I ask you to gently confront your mind and body with visualising 'I am a miracle of life and I deserve love.' Stop deserving self-hatred; it will not serve you, your family and friends, it will be unlikely to attract to you a partner who loves who they are. If life is a mirror it will only attract somebody who does not love him or herself, and then the negative cycle goes on again.

BECOMING PARTNERS

I suggest you read Carl Rogers 'Becoming Partners', the chapter called, "Three marriages and one growing person". This for me, has such honest self-disclosure from a woman called Irene about her childhood, the creation of her self-concept, the elements of bad and good relationships, and about bizarre sexual rationalisations she made to get what she thought was love. Then as she changes her self-concept, from being unlovable to deserving love from deep inside, we see her accepting all of herself including the 'black bits' without condemnation. When I first read this chapter 23 years ago I cried and sobbed deeply for the person who was lost inside me, who was unloved and felt unlovable, yet Irene helped me see what was possible if I started to go within and become more honest with me. As she talked to Carl she said, "These are questions from me to me... What is it you really want? ...What is it that you're looking for? And the answer turned out not to be married, not to have six children, not to live happily ever after, at all. It turned out to be that I wanted to learn how to love someone, just one person, and to be loved, and that's all." Then later "I had a great talk with myself, and felt a sense of peace that I'd never experienced before in my life.... The peace I felt about myself and the good feelings I had towards me and my own private joy were obvious." Consequently she attracted to her a man who loved himself from a deeper consciousness that helped her awareness grow.

BEGIN YOUR HONEST TALK WITH YOU NOW
There is a point, it can come on our deathbed or it can come during our life now, where we have an honest talk with ourselves, where we drop criticism and we begin to learn COMPASSION for other people and ourselves. By compassion I mean an inner empathy with ourselves. Then we can allow others to get close to us, and we radiate an awareness that does not judge. The power within sparks a flame of new intelligence, forgiveness and insight. Barriers to loving you and others fall away and you know you are *"lovable because you exist"*.

Cease to be fascinated by your horror story, make up your mind to stop telling it to everyone don't keep carrying it around with you. Write and tell it then let it go with love. Your and my hurt is not you and I; we are so much more. Live now today, you are the product of the choices you are making now, when I understood this, new energy flowed through my whole being. Make 'healing you' your business, we can have as many new perceptions as we like, for example, How many of you know the following intellectually:

• It's good to eat good food and exercise daily.

• It's good to meditate daily for twenty minutes.

• Pray and bless your food with love.

• Give up blame.

• Stop living in the past.

• Stop speaking your pain and wounds.

• Read positive books and listen to tapes etc.

We may know these and much more, yet to convert these from an intellectual perception to a whole body mind experience I believe you have to forgo being comfortable, and drop your excuses. You and I need to make a deep commitment to heal. To get up early, read, meditate, do an exercise you enjoy, listen to those tapes, write your affirmations, and let the presence inside us know we are here and mean business to grow and change. Then your life will change in mind, body and spirit without guilt. Please don't wait until a crisis comes to make the change. 'DO IT NOW'.

Keeping myself honest as honest as I am able with all my blind spots is a vital ingredient to living in the now and having fantastic love! I will try to say to my partner. "You must be mad, how can you love me?" Then I laugh at the old critical tape beginning to play inside my head and I let this old message go and let love run through my mind, it is so much better than being critical or wanting approval. The more honest our sharing the more compassion I experience from the power within and the more energy and balance I have for everything I do and say in life. MY GOOD COMES FROM EVERYWHERE AND EVERYONE. And so it is.

THE POWERS OF OUR MIND

"Compared with what we ought to be, we are only half awake. We are making use of only a small part of our mental and physical resources. Stating the thing broadly, the human individual thus far lives within his limits. He possesses powers of various sorts which he habitually fails to use."

William James

The father of American Psychology also thought 90 percent of us is only using 10 percent of our mind power. In terms of energy modern psychologists estimate that we use only 1/10 of 1 percent of our energies and powers. The rest of our forces are expressed outward instead of inward. Two thousand years ago, the great physician Jesus, tried to point out the source of man's unlimited indwelling powers when he said to the Pharisees,

"The Kingdom of God is within you."

Luke 17:20

I believe there is a divine current of energy within you and me that carries healing power of every conceivable kind. Our energy flows where our attention is directed. Yet this energy has to be guided and directed in our bodies by our higher intelligence. How do we communicate with this intelligence? By the thoughts, we choose and what we say, so what we think and say releases energy throughout our bodies. If that thought is negative it will release exactly that in our bodies. However, if we are willing to communicate to the miracle with thoughts that are positive, loving and forgiving, we will bring a healing power to bear on all levels, physical, mental, emotional and spiritual.

IDENTIFY YOUR DEEP PATTERNS SO YOU CAN RECLAIM YOUR LIFE

This may be correct in theory, yet difficult to achieve in practice when the emotional trauma runs deep, let me shed a little light. A little more about me, that may show you the reader how arrested the powers of our mind can become on all these levels. When I was between 2 and 15 years old, my mother and father would fight in so many ways and the rage that surfaced would boil over into real fear of losing my father and mother. One day a frightened seven-year-old boy found his mother half-conscious on returning from church. The incident left me with a deep scar of fear and rage taken in, at first I thought I had done some dreadful deed that made her so angry to hurt her self. Then as I listened to my sisters and my mother shouting I realised my father was with another woman and that my mother wanted to end her life. She went into mental hospital where she received ECT (electric convulsive treatment). On her return I can remember she could hardly recognise me, I vowed I would care for my mother for the rest of my life.

At this point my life went inward and I collapsed, I secretly hated my father; I wanted to kill him and love him at the same time I would have huge rages in my mind, I did not understand he was doing the best with the knowledge he had. Yet I was unconscious of how angry I was at my mother attempting to abandon me, of her love. However inadequate and conditional that love was, I wanted my mother's love and I would do anything to keep her alive, and I would make up for my father's mistakes. This feeling and thinking pattern took me on a journey of half a lifetime to work through.

Now I love my father and mother and see them in a new light, they were the right parents for me to learn certain lessons. Did I choose them? Maybe, perhaps they chose me; this may seem a difficult notion to swallow; yet if we are here to learn and advance our spiritual soul, maybe we were perfect for each other for the lessons to be learnt. I ask myself "if life is a mirror, why have I attracted to me so many angry people in my life, especially women who hate men? And why have I spent days and years listening to women who have been a victim to men or vice versa? This is not written to make you feel sorry for me, it's time for me to get some clearer insight on me and hopefully to help you see how stuck our lives can become in an old event that hurt our fragile inner child and drains our power to live now.

So a whole personality and career can be built around a trauma in our childhood that keeps us stuck. In many ways it's like an old record that keeps replaying the same tune, only revamped at various stages of time, first on 78's, then onto 45's, then to tapes, then eventually to compact discs, each time the tune updated. This is not to denigrate my life and the choices I have made, yet I do see how my mind came to be stuck in a child trying to work out how to appease my mother's and father's needs for loving who they were. I not only parented them, I lost the ability to see and think clearly in my mind. So I see that life has kept attracting to me relationships and situations that have old unanswered issues deeply entrenched in my subconscious mind.

It is no wonder that so many of us use such a small capacity of our brain when our conscious mind is dancing to an old crackled tune from the subconscious. Perhaps you may have some old tunes stopping you seeing more clearly. So when we start to ask the question "How do I love me? How can I really love a God? Who is this God that allows such suffering? How can I love my neighbour as myself with all our blind spots?" I am going to attempt a possible answer by talking about the mind.

NEW KNOWLEDGE AND AWARENESS HELPS
US LEAP IN CONSCIOUSNESS

Reading books on the mind may help you, "The Science of Mind" by Ernest Holmes. Dr Jean Houston in her foreword states "This is a book for the ages. It contains the distilled wisdom of many eras, many cultures, and one great soul. To read it is ...to enter into partnership with God, to relearn the laws of co-creation." This one book can help each of us, to quote Ernest, relearn, "The Divine Plan is one of freedom, bondage is not God-ordained. Freedom is the birthright of every living soul. All instinctively feel this. The truth points to freedom, under law. Thus the inherent nature of man is seeking to express itself in terms of freedom. We do well to listen to this Inner Voice, for it tells us of a life wonderful in its scope; of a love beyond our fondest dreams; of a freedom which the soul craves." And a little later asks, "What is the mind? No man living knows. We know a great deal about the mind, but not what it is. By mind we mean consciousness. We are now using it.... All we know about it is not what it is, but what it does." Ernest clearly states, "When we learn to trust the universe, we shall be happy, prosperous and well." So the more we seek a relationship with the universal mind, God, through using our conscious mind positively, intelligently and with trust we will dissolve our ignorance of the true nature of reality.

"TO LEARN HOW TO THINK IS TO LEARN HOW TO LIVE, for our thoughts go into a medium that is Infinite in its ability to do and be." Then Ernest gives a little key that shifts our consciousness, his masculine use of words I would like to change, however he wrote this in the 1920's. "Man, by thinking, can bring into his experience whatsoever he desires if he thinks correctly, and becomes a living embodiment of his thoughts. This is not done by holding thoughts but by knowing the Truth." This is: "ALL THOUGHT IS CREATIVE." So "within us, then, there is a creative field, which we call the subjective mind; around us there is a creative field which we call Subjective. One is universal and the other is individual, but in reality they are one." Then he states emphatically "THERE IS ONE MENTAL LAW IN THE UNIVERSE, AND WHERE WE USE IT, IT BECOMES OUR LAW BECAUSE WE INDIVIDUALISED IT." Simply put what we give out goes into a law of mind and comes back, multiplied. Then he states what I felt or intuitively knew and you the reader may know. "It is impossible to plumb the depths of the individual, because the individual mind is really not individual but is individualised." So he concludes, "Behind the individual is the Universal, which has no limits. In this concept alone lies the possibility of eternal and endless expansion. Everyone is universal on the subjective side of life, and individual only at the point of conscious perception. The riddle is solved, and we all use the creative power of the Universal Mind every time we use our own mind."

So if all thought is creative here we are dealing with a law not a whim, a fancy, there are no excuses, great is the subconscious mind yet it is "Set in motion by the conscious thought." So our road to freedom "Is not mysterious". The more we choose thoughts in our conscious mind that are open and receptive to love and trust the more the Universal Mind, "the Over-Soul, or the Eternal Spirit which we call God 'will' reveal itself to whoever is receptive to it". So we are living in a "spiritual universe", which "must be one of pure Intelligence and perfect life, dominated by Love, by Reason and by the power to create." So often my clients come thinking that God will not forgive them, this holds their past as though it's the present. Once the mind thinks and feels mistakes can be truly dissolved by coming daily to the Spirit of goodness for a complete washing away of all mistakes, fears and troubles, they are in a far better psychological, physical and spiritual health to open themselves to a God of loving thoughts.

"The key to this door is held in the mind of Intelligence, working in accordance with the universal law. Through experience, man learns what is really good and satisfying, what is truly satisfying, what is truly worthwhile. As his intelligence increases, and his capacity to understand the subtle laws of Nature grow, he will gradually be set free. As he learns the Truth, the Truth will automatically free him". I then love how he says the following *"God is always God. No matter what our emotional storm, or what our objective situation, may be, there is always something hidden in the inner being that has never been violated"*. In the most abused people I have counselled I have found this. "We may stumble, but always there is that Eternal Voice, forever whispering within our ear, that thing which for-ever sings and sings".

I see simply our subconscious (subjective) mind is merged with God, the Divine Infinite and Universal mind. However our conscious mind feeds our subconscious mind, so if we choose conscious thoughts of hate, criticism, fear, and guilt the subconscious mind feeds that back to our conscious intelligence and the law of mind will create that in our experience. However if we start to trust, love and forgive and dissolve the negative, the subconscious will receive abundant love and good we cannot imagine from the universal mind. Then the truth that all thought is creative will be revealed to us as natural and spontaneous and we have within us an individual divine nature, waiting to synchronise and understand God within us. Ernest ends his first chapter; "The mind, which we discover within us, is the Mind that governs everything. This is the Thing Itself, and we should recognise its simplicity." I make no apologies for quoting from "The Science of Mind", I hope you will read it.

HEALING SECRETS

Now I move onto Catherine Ponder's books called "The Healing secrets of the Ages", plus "The Dynamic laws of Healing". In these books she shares the healing secrets "known and invoked by the great minds down through the ages". Her book simply relays the "12 mind powers "located within the vital nerve centres in your body, which greatly affect your health, either constructively or destructively, depending how you use these mind powers." She goes on to state, "I first learned of these secret teachings when I took up the study of practical Christianity and heard these mind powers described as 'the 12 powers of man'. Their mystical significance is linked with Jesus and his twelve disciples....". As you read her book you will discover that each dis-ease "always has a mental correspondent with one of the 12 mind powers located in the body."

The relationship between our mind and body is a vital ingredient to learn about. For me discovering the divine super conscious phase of my mind is like discovering what Paul said to the Romans:

"Be ye transformed by the renewing of your mind"
Romans 12:2

The super conscious mind is situated in the crown of the head, it can be described as the Christ mind or what the Sufis call 'the Friend, Hindus call 'the Divine Mother', mystic Jews call 'Shekinah', Tibetan Buddhists relate to this as 'Tara'. It is the 'I am', the centre of intelligence and wisdom, since it has direct access to universal life and wisdom. Your intuitive flashes of perception, hunches or extrasensory perception powers function from this area. Miracles often occur when this Divine Intelligence is activated.

ACTIVATING YOUR SUPERCONSCIOUS MIND

Thinking and saying positive divine affirmations is speaking to the intelligence that made us in a language that is intelligent and totally loving and begins our healing. Consciously developing Divine inter-dependence is through activating our super conscious mind by devotional prayer, meditation and through spiritual study. So often we do our life on our own, that the idea of yielding to a higher intelligence within can seem like a loss of power. Yet this resistance comes from our feeling unworthy. So many of us have a false belief in a punishing God from fearful theologies that create toxic shame and guilt. What if God is a universal power of total love and we are his or her beloved child. Then if we communicate intelligently, sensitively and with a deep sincere devotion of loving ourselves as the miracle we are, the only power that awaits you and that answers you is the power of love and forgiveness.

As we choose thoughts and speak those thoughts to this inner power that made us in total love, the intelligence creator will make us a

channel of love, healing, joy, forgiveness and a creator of practical dreams for real peace and harmony on this earth. We can change the world by dissolving deep-rooted thinking and feeling patterns and learning to love the miracle we are. As soon as we begin dissolving criticism, resentment, fear and guilt, and replace these old patterns with thoughts and feelings of forgiveness and love, then our soul will join with others on this path, which I believe is becoming far more travelled. In each one of us is a miracle, a unique human being, waiting to be unfolded to our true spiritual nature. "Life has to be guided by intelligence" according to Myrtle Fillimore's secret in healing herself from tuberculosis in 1886. "Life is simply a form of energy, and has to be guided and directed by this intelligence. How do we communicate with intelligence?
By thinking and talking of course". She lived a further 40 years!

Affirming "Divine Intelligence" awakens the power of the super conscious mind and then unites it with the conscious mind in the forehead. The combined intelligence of both is released into the subconscious mind located in your abdominal region of the body. Dr. Emmet Fox explains in his booklet, The Seven Aspects of God. *"You should treat yourself for wisdom and intelligence at least two or three times a week, by thinking about intelligence and claiming it for yourself"*.

When you get an intuitive thought to do or not to do something, follow through without talking. Kahlil Gibran in The prophet explained: *"You talk when you cease to be at peace with your thoughts...and in much of your talking, thinking is half murdered"*. The more you study the power of thought, the more you will choose words carefully, you will talk less and think more and you must be independent of the opinion of others. Then your intuitive divine intelligence will serve you. Catherine Ponder states: "Remember this about intuitive knowing: It will always lead you into greater good provided you follow it quietly and nonresistantly, rather than questioning it, trying to reason it through, or talking to others about it." Read Proverbs 3. The words permeate our hearts.

DYNAMIC LAWS OF HEALING

In Catherine Ponder's second book on healing she states; "Most people have not yet learned the healing secret of the ages-that health is basically an inside job, mentally as well as physically. No matter how successful a treatment is in times of illness, a person often becomes sick again and again, because he has not gotten at the cause of his illness ill thoughts and feelings about himself, others, his creator, and the world in which he lives. These ill thoughts constrict the life force within him, causing disease, or lack of ease". People need order in their thinking, emotions, bodies and lives. The powers of the mind are not just located in the brain; it is located in every cell of your body. I encourage you to read Louise Hay's little book "Heal Your Body" and the "Anatomy of the Spirit" by Dr Caroline Myss, which will help you connect mind, body and spirit even further and realise insights on healing and your spiritual centres. So the strongest thing in your body is your thinking! "As a man thinketh so is he". It has been stated that one healthy thought persistently expressed dissolves 1,000 negative thoughts. Catherine says, "It is habitual wrong thoughts, deep hates, secret resentments, and wrong prejudices that play such havoc with health."

Our natural state, our wisdom, our higher intelligence is biased toward health. Do not criticise your body as evil, fat, thin, disabled, useless and unimportant. So often I hear "I must be bad, it's Gods will for me to be sick." Or "I must be a 'bad' Christian!" God is seen as a punishing God. If God is really loving thoughts it is truly possible to love God our neighbour and ourselves without feeling guilty for loving ourselves, it will help us know God rather than know about God and know our neighbour, with a truer love, this will manifest a great destiny for us all. You do not have to go through hell here, to get to heaven. Maybe it's time to understand the gift of loving thoughts of forgiveness and what still may block your healing.

> '*HEAVEN IS HERE, THERE IS NO OTHER PLACE*
> *HEAVEN IS NOW, THERE IS NO OTHER TIME.*'
>
> A course in Miracles.

EXERCISE

Look into a mirror and ask... "What negative thoughts do I have about my body?"

• Write them down.

• Where and who did I learn these from?

• Then ask yourself - Are you willing to release and let those thoughts go, or do you want to hold onto them?

CHAPTER 11
Soul Talk Creates Conscious Freedom

"Forgiveness with consciousness is the key to find love. Yet your 'NO' from the past maybe inside your soul mind, and this needs to come out to open your heart to loving the miracle you are and healing you & our planet."

"Freedom" is a big word and as an idea it has responsibility, which means taking back our power. How often have you thought, "I want to be free from the past"? Then followed this with a negative thought in your mind of yourself or another, or of the world and locking yourself in that past hurt, and then blaming self or others. Yet what you are thinking right now determines your future. For people who have been violated, rejected and abused, the word "forgiveness" is not in their vocabulary. When you have been too frightened to say "No" to your abusers, you have not learned your "NO" power. This "NO" power is a divine power of life and can reconnect you to the miracle of love inside you. We can free ourselves from so many troubles, past, present and future if we learn to say "NO" with passion and say "NO" to other peoples opinions that have imprisoned us. If we carry a secret "NO" inside of us, the intimacy of experiencing forgiveness and love are always kept at arms length.

For years I have listened to the tortured soul of peoples lives from their past or present and when they cannot say "NO" to the people who have haunted them and mean it, it's like a whole life force is missing in them. When I cannot say "NO" and mean it, I leak my power to live how I am meant to live now. If I cannot say "YES" to life and mean "YES" I feel in "NO PERSONS LAND", no matter how I try to forgive I will hold the secret resentment in the cells of my body and mind and create dis-ease somewhere in my temple. Yet I am doing the best I can at the time and with the awareness I have.

MENTAL AND EMOTIONAL HOUSECLEANING

When you are in a hard place, you may be unable to gently pray or say, "I FORGIVE" once or twice. It's time to say "NO" to whatever you don't want and say "YES" to what you do want. The passionate "NO" will release ideas of what really went on in your past, then you can begin to heal and connect to what you do want. The more your "NO" means "NO"; the power within will give you thoughts of a vital creative energy. Then this affirmation will be a dynamic law in your universe. "AS I SAY YES TO LIFE THEN LIFE SAYS YES TO ME". You cannot deny your feelings and emotions, yet you are no longer at their mercy, you don't give them energy when they surface the thoughts don't drown you. You may even laugh at how fixed you were in punishing you, yet you know you were doing your best with what you knew. Healing in every area of your mind and body will reconnect to the genius wonder child; an inner critical parent will no longer parent you. Tiredness will be replaced with creative energy and your daily positive affirmations will be your new reality. Then all you need is to be willing to forgive and the universe will bring the "How"?

In my own path to forgiving I needed to learn that I subconsciously rejected my own healing. Somewhere I internalised that I was unworthy of being healed, there was a pattern of thinking and feeling below the obvious that made me cling onto my hurt. My conscious mind had done the best it could to survive and protect me. I could not say "Yes" or "No" and mean them. I felt anger was so wrong. In my self-rejection I had learned to reject good for me which kept me powerless, yet it helped me survive. It took being lovingly confronted by my therapist and people who loved me to help me mentally accept the good I desired and deserved. I no longer wanted to hang on to emotions of dis-ease and the attention and sympathy that accompany it. I did not want to keep leading my life with my wounds, however unconscious. This affirmation may help raise your consciousness:

"I am willing to release the past and forgive everyone including myself. I now know and accept I was doing the best with what I was conscious of at the time. I create my future now by choosing love and forgiveness of others and myself. I take responsibility for my life now."

SOUL TALK CREATES FREEDOM INSIDE AND OUT

To say "I forgive..." whoever hurt you into a mirror, looking into your eyes is hard, yet it immediatly tells you your barriers to loving yourself. As you keep doing this exercise a new awareness dawns that helps you think and see clearly. As I began to work with a mirror, I saw each person who hurt me differently, they were seeking love too, yet had no idea 'How?' It felt like a new emotional and mental clarity came into my conscious thoughts. I could see more clearly and think about those who hurt me in a new light. I saw their deep patterns of hurt and pain. Blaming words gradually ceased and now if I blame it's like a small electric shock passes through my body, I get headaches, pain somewhere in my body, it's like my body will not lie even when my mind tries to camouflage the truth. I am learning to be confronted with my blind spots without thinking "I am a bad person."

FORGIVING IGNITES OUR DIVINE SPARK

As you forgive, the blueprint of your divine spark will ignite healing in you. Perception and understanding will grow; you will look at the flowers, the sky, and the people who walk past you with a deeper awareness. Your love of life will be renewed, your inner child will play and create in every area of your life, and you will let go and flow in the moment even when life gets tough your highest good will be served. Your energy will enhance your compassion and creativity in all areas.

There are so many examples of people who have forgiven their tormenters, including themselves. In areas of extreme conflict some will stay hurt, while others have a far deeper understanding through forgiving. Each time a person forgives it's like seeds of love are sown inside the hearts of the human mind somewhere on this planet. People who go beyond their story of pain, who learn from the power within and reconnect to the miracle they are, become blessed by choosing thoughts that create life and love from their heart, joy becomes real not just a word.

CHOOSE TO READ & LISTEN TO GOOD NEWS AND THE UNIVERSE WILL CREATE MORE GOOD NEWS

With war and famine often being talked about on our news, I ask you to choose reading and listening to positive news, subscribe to www.positivenews.net and concentrate your mind on practical dreams that are coming true, where positive divine consciousness within individuals is being translated into economic and political realities. Soul talk that is honest talk creates freedom in the mind; personal growth is not a selfish act. Love with compassion cannot just stop within the individual we are all joined by our souls and then "soul freedom" permeates all relationships and creation. We heal our planet when we love and heal our self, the universal mind notices. And so it is.

HOW TO LOVE YOURSELF

I have just left a man who was going to commit suicide a year ago. He said, *"My mother has rung up and told me she loved me! A better Christmas present I could not wish for"*. He is learning to know he is loveable because he exists and to love all parts of what has made him unique and gradually shedding beliefs that do not support him. The miracle that shines in his energy radiates in his body, language and his relationships. This man made a conscious decision to live and learn to love himself and give thanks for everything. He could have chosen to leave the planet early. As this individual has come to appreciate himself as a miracle of life, he is appreciating how much he has to live for and what he has to give.

BUILDING A DIVINE SPARK INTO A LOVING LIGHT

In order to bring about any positive results with your growth or with anything you need to persist repeating loving positive thoughts. You must mean business; constantly reiterate the thought until it becomes a positive habit. Think how long you chose negative and self-defeating habits, you learnt those by constant repetition. Catch yourself doing your life well, and go up to any mirror and congratulate yourself. Instead of catching yourself doing something wrong, you could say:

"Well done for getting it, you really are bright."

Then give thanks. I have just been playing with a one-year-old child and they were preening as I took time to just be with them, and give them my full attention, she loved being loved and so did I!

"If I have repeated myself in this book I do not apologise, I want the principles to loving you to be caught as well as taught."

THE HOW

1. Learn: How the mind and body works. Stop choosing thoughts that hurt you and others. Even when you do criticise, learn the lesson of forgiving yourself and the person who you are blaming.

2. Practice daily present tense positive affirmations, into a mirror and see your resistance as a key to your freedom. Thank the negative for sharing and move on by releasing them. Write them, speak them and listen to tapes anywhere and anytime, especially in the morning and evening. Remember the invisible law of mind, that when you think a thought it goes out into the universe and comes back multiplied and creates your experience. There is such power in starting an affirmation with the word "Divine".

3. Stop frightening your mind with thoughts that create fear and guilt. Learn to be gentle with your mind and body and realise they are totally connected. If you have lots of old anger, learn to release it safely and build intelligent ways to loving all ages within you. Allow the child within to give you natural intelligence and vitality; coupled with a nurturing parent, your adult will thrive even when life gets tough. This will attract more healing and you will make intelligent decisions, and if it's a mistake you can change it.

4. Meditate and/or pray on a daily basis, silence slows down our thoughts (we cannot stop them) and let the power communicate to our busy minds. Do it your way, make it simple. We have made meditation so complex when it can be so simple. I meditate while walking, windsurfing and gardening, as well as when sitting quietly.

5. Support yourself by choosing good friends and know that each person's energy we are around can replenish or drain us. Affirm positive work, time, money, partners and home and give thanks for everything in your life, then more good will come into your experience of life.

6. Join or start a self-empowerment group, where you can share and learn together to a simple structure all the latest knowledge.

7. Look after you, learn what your body is telling you. Learn about your body and attract to you the right food, exercise and people who love you just for you being you and make clear affirmations on your health. I have learnt to visit all types of holistic medical practitioners, Suzy my dietician and reflexologist has helped me look after me, without guilt.

8. Love your inner child and all ages within you. Develop a nurturing forgiving inner parent and your child will grow into the miracle it has always been from when first conceived. The child and parent can create a great adult! You will magnetise to you new opportunities, skills, jobs and relationships.

9. Take back your power and be honest with yourself. Look carefully at what you are attracting to you; remember life is a mirror. Is the life you have now what you truly want? Read books like "Be Your Own Life coach" by Fiona Harold, this may help you look at your true talents and give you a structure to achieve what you want. Or visit my friend Karin Peterson-Sitrin on her website www.possibilitiesinaction.com

10. Read and listen to tapes and be prepared to learn and study. Do the work and have fun. It is lovely to spend time reading and receiving insights from people whom role model ideas for intelligent and practical living.

11. DO IT NOW- THE POINT OF POWER IS IN THE PRESENT MOMENT. Remember "One of the great secrets of establishing healthy relationships with others is to learn how to clear inharmonious ideas about them from your own thinking." How? "Ancient minds of all ages felt that every person has an angel or higher self. They felt that when you cannot reach that person through reasoning... you could reach his higher self by writing to his angel. They believed that the angel of God's Presence is a miracle working presence that is available to everyone. By writing to a person's angel, you establish in your own thinking a harmonious feeling about that person.... There is something about written words that reach past the emotional blocks of vanity, ego, pride, deception, intellectual argumentativeness, hurt feelings, inferiority, and that reach deep within to the judgement seat of such people, penetrating their spiritual nature." Catherine Ponder "The Dynamic Laws of Healing".

Here are a few thoughts from the Dalai Lama, which are just above my head while I type, with some of my personal reflections.

• *"Take into account that great love and great achievements involve great risk"*. It is a great lesson of love to write this book although I risk rejection. Risking being open about me could bring your rejection. If I dwelt upon this thought I would never of started, yet whatever the outcome it has been a privilege to learn so much.

• *"When you lose, don't lose the lesson"*. I lost a chapter on this creative computer the other day, after a scream, I then said "It will work out for my highest good." Then I learnt all sorts of skills about my computer from a friend Keith, who drops round when anything stops. I give him help, while he helps me, what a great way to learn lessons.

- *"Follow the three R's: Respect for self, respect for others, responsibility for all your actions."* The more I respect me the more I can genuinely respect others who differ from me in their point of view, and take full responsibility for how I react.

- *"Remember that not getting what you want is sometimes a wonderful stroke of luck."* I wanted to go windsurfing in north Wales this summer; the family wasn't convinced it was for them. Suddenly a thought came and I found an old phone number in Crete, we went there and all of us had the best holiday.

- *"Don't let a little dispute injure a great friendship."* A few days ago I was hurt by something said to me, I went out into the fields and let the anger out safely, and then we talked and began to see what was going on, it helped us both grow.

- *"When you realise you've made a mistake, take immediate steps."* I bought a kite and tore it when trying to put it together, took it back to the shop, yet failed to mention the tiny tear. That afternoon went windsurfing and ripped my sail. I knew the universe was telling me something. I went straight back and admitted my omission. They received my apologies with grace and it was complete, they would not take my money.

- *"Spend some time alone every day."* To walk or sit quietly and listen and learn silence is so refreshing, especially when I ask to see and hear clearly. Thoughts come later just when I need them. Even when I do the washing up I can do it with love, if I decide to (do it with love).

- *"Open your arms to change but don't let go of your values."* I now love opening my arms and saying, "I am open and receptive to all good." That lets my love of life sing inside my heart, with a value that's priceless.

- *"Remember that silence is sometimes the best answer."* Sitting opposite people who are in pain, the less I say the more love I feel and it shows. Often they have talked for 99% of the time, and they thank me for all that I have said, they feel so much better. Perhaps I say a lot of love with my silence.

- *"Live a good, honourable life. Then when you get older and think back, you'll be able to enjoy it a second time."* As I learn the power of thought and the law of mind the sooner I have become more honest with me and discovering the miracle within, has helped me live congruently and transparently, even my children notice!

- *"A loving atmosphere in your home is the foundation for your life."* To come home spiritually, mentally, emotionally and physically ignites a flame of real hope for love to radiate wherever you are.

- *"In disagreements with loved ones, deal only with the current situation. Don't bring up the past"*. This was one big lesson for me, I used to know exactly what buttons I could push, and it makes life horrible. If I do it now I say I am sorry and mean it.

- *"Once a year, go someplace you've never been before"*. You don't need to travel far just see things through other people's eyes that radiate love. If each of us is God's lens on this planet then we can travel each day to places you have never been before, and it's great to travel. I have a growing friendship with a man who travels to places where women are kept in prostitution; he smuggles them out, and gives them help to take back their lives. I salute people who put their love to work for bigger causes than themselves.

- *"Remember that the best relationship is one in which your love for each other exceeds your need for each other"*. Going within and finding deep love that breaks you from co-dependant love, (a needy love), is a gift to bring to any partner you attract and grow to love.

- *"Judge your success by what you had to give up in order to get it"*. Working at something I love, that serves growth and healing, allows me to give up certain comforts yet the benefits are leaps in consciousness and vitality. Now I give thanks for what I give up to find real gems of wisdom and manifesting my destiny.

- *"Approach love and cooking with reckless abandon"*. I love this instruction! I am learning to cook with love, the food tastes so much better.

"Is there a rebel in us all?" I remember my Buddhist teacher saying, "You did it your way and what did you learn?" I enjoyed the thrill of stepping outside rules at school, yet I never took responsibility, I always blamed and tried to be innocent. If now I break the rules I can laugh and cry at the same time, and just see a little further up the mountain of life. This time I take responsibility and enjoy the journey of receiving and giving.

CHAPTER 12
What is the purpose of it all?

"Every day envision the world at peace. Each of us well fed with physical and soulful food. Knowing despite our circumstances that we are connected to divine love and forgiveness. We connect on all levels to each other as miracles of light and our love disolves the dark. And so it is."

Going within to connect to our higher self, we learn to forgive and love those who have hurt us, primarily ourselves. A rebirth of a miracle baby is ignited in each of us. Just like a baby we relearn our meaning and purpose through thinking thoughts of pure love, trust and a deeper forgiveness becomes possible. At first there is resistance yet this time our inner awareness, which some call intuition, knows and needs love, a deep respectful love. Despite our past there is a point where through becoming more honest with ourselves we can consciously choose to let the past go and live in the present, we see and experience that past as positive fuel to love ourselves and life, instead of beating ourselves up and blaming parents or others. Each day we learn to go within to connect to our divine guidance, that is loving thoughts, we then attract to ourselves increasingly creative loving thoughts to consciously realise we are a miracle and that each moment of life is unfolding miracles of love.

No matter how negative the past our mind becomes like good soil where we plant loving seeds that reflect our unique talents. Our patience increases as we learn from every situation and relationship. Even when we struggle to love, the paradoxes from past, present or future no longer stop us learning. Our old beliefs no longer hold us back, like the rigid beliefs of fear, anger, guilt and criticism that were our daily diet. Our affirmations and positive thoughts breathe through us like strong winds of healing. Our consciousness deepens with words that give life to our physical and spiritual healing. As we grow our "Inner Light" grows, through prayerful meditation; people are attracted to us at exactly the right time. People open their lives to us on buses and trains, wherever we go. We will attract to us a teacher or a spiritual director, books will leap off the shelf and we are open to learning from them, our past addictions no longer hold us.

SOUL TO SOUL

We connect to souls that are finding their miracle, and make deep connections for peace and healing. We find the gate and knock and the door is opened, where the fruit tree of false knowledge is left untouched. We know it feeds us lies, and we let it go with love. On a humorous yet meaningful note, a lady minister from my church, passed this to me:

THE PURPLE HAT

"Age 3 She looks at herself and sees a Queen.

Age 8 She looks at herself and sees Cinderella.

Age 15 She looks at herself and sees an Ugly Sister (Mum I can't go to school like this).

Age 20 She looks at herself and sees "too fat/too thin/too short/too tall/too straight/too curly-but decides she's going out anyway.

Age 30 She looks at herself and sees too fat/too thin too short/ too tall too straight/too curly and decides she doesn't have time to fix it so she's going out anyway.

Age 40 She looks at herself and sees "clean" and goes out anyway.

Age 50 she looks at herself and sees "I am" and goes wherever she wants to go.

Age 60 She looks at herself and reminds herself of all the people who can't even see themselves in the mirror anymore. Goes out and conquers the world.

Age 70 She looks at herself and sees wisdom, laughter and ability and goes out and enjoys life.

Age 80 Doesn't bother to look. Just puts on the purple hat and goes out to have fun with the world".

Author unknown

What is the purpose of life on this earth? To become "attuned" with the miracle that made us, for me that is God, loving thoughts, and love our neighbour, as a miracle and love ourselves as a miracle. At death we no longer fear or sense shame, we go to meet the love that made us with love. Only now we breathe love within light. I encourage you to go within and connect to the miracle you are by loving who you truly are. Enjoy the journey and share your journey with us all, and help heal this heaven on earth.

CREATING AN AFFIRMATION

I have just left a young man who asked me to help him create thoughts that would build the life he truly wanted. Here are some practical "Laws" and "How to's". Remember you are putting your thoughts out into a law of mind that will give you whatever you think and say. It will come back to you as experience. If we think and say "I am no good, nobody loves me", that is what the law of mind will give you in experience. Now imagine saying what you truly want with creative loving intentions and creative loving words, you will receive back from this universal mind exactly what you are thinking and speaking with interest. Your deep intention that is in your subconscious mind will be examined by the universal mind. So the more you repeat consciously the positive thought to your subconscious mind for example:

"I love and approve of myself exactly as I am".
"I am a channel for divine ideas".
"I am divinely protected and guided".

The more you say these affirmations the more you mean business, and you begin to water down your resistance, from your past. Then you believe what you are saying, the universal mind notices. Remember this law of mind, the universal source; God is a living loving creative entity. The "Thing itself" I believe wants us to think and speak to "it" lovingly not just from our pain.

How to:

1. Sit quietly, go inside and slow your thoughts down and say this: "I am a channel for divine ideas to flow through me", then ask yourself and the universal mind. "What is it I need to learn?", "What is it that I could do?", "What do I have to give?" Then just wait, you may do a simple meditation, on the in breath say "for" on the out breath say

"peace" or "love" or "give". Each time your mind wanders just come back to the simple statement.

2. Be patient and see what thoughts you find yourself thinking during or after the meditation. Write them down in a journal, the ideas may pop up as you go to sleep or as you wake up, mine often do.

3. Then as the thoughts come like: "Heal your life", "learn new skills", "become a writer", "clean the house", "Learn to love yourself", "start a business", " move house", "create a new job". Just become aware and see what the universe is dropping into your mind.

4. Then write each thought on a spider chart, then intuitively mind storm the values and qualities of those thoughts. An example: Become a writer

As you build your web of ideas you fill in the values and qualities the intuitive self is receiving, then you begin to see what affirmations you need and the right words will form in your mind. For example, I built this affirmation gradually:

"The creativity of the universe directs me to exactly the right people, books tapes and resources to learn and write and publish these ideas. They all come at the right time and in the perfect space sequence."

Which is like saying the command to the "cosmic chef", please start cooking this order. Thank you. Then I sit and go within and listen, up pops:

"I write with the divine intention guiding me and expressing love and forgiveness."

These are all values and qualities my higher self is suggesting.

"I am open to learning what and how to write."

"I am open and receptive to new ideas from the past and present. I see and think clearly."

Gradually I am building my truly positive thoughts, which is becoming my new belief. Resistance may come up, "you can't be a writer! Nobody wants to know what you have to say". So I immediately turn this into the opposite by thanking them for sharing and then say,

"Divine love expresses itself through me now."

I move on, don't stay stuck with old beliefs. Then sit and write the affirmations, one of the affirmations that gradually built inside me for this book, the inner child affirmation cards and CD is this:

"I am open and receptive to divine ideas, they come to me at the right time and in the perfect space sequence. The creativity of the universe expresses through me now. The books, affirmation cards and CD's are created with love. All are written, spoken, edited, illustrated, typed, published, printed and retailed by loving people. They bless everyone with love, peace, healing and prosperity of every kind and new insights to re-connecting us to the universal mind and contribute to world harmony. And so it is".

I have just read out this chapter to my children, they clapped, that was lovely. I hope you catch the ideas of building your affirmations. A friend has just given me "The Right to Write" by Julia Cameron, wonderful; do get this book if you want to write, thank you universe. Briefly my suggestions are:
  Meditate-ask simple questions and then wait. As ideas come write them down, then make a mind map around the idea. Then build simple present tense loving positively worded affirmations and keep passing the affirmations through your mind and soul. This lets God know you have heard, and you mean business with wonderful, truly magnificent miracles unfolding within and without. You will also get images, one image came into my mind was of a sunflower and I just started doodling then it gradually evolved into a metaphor for the growing miracle of the book. Remember keep-giving thanks and you will be blessed with more good. Thank you. And so it is.

EVERYTHING WE GIVE OUT COMES BACK
It can seem that we go a little forward and a little back as we learn to love ourselves. I woke up this morning thinking negative, lots of self-doubt about the book and will anybody want to read it. Then I thought:

- 'Go and meditate' which I did then the dog got up licking my hand and wanting me to play with him.
- Then the thought came 'I must get the children up for school', so I stop meditating.
- Then I looked in the fridge and saw how dirty it was and beat myself up for not cleaning it.
- Then as I waited for the porridge to cook, it burnt! As I started my Yoga, the dog decided to join in.
- The children were late getting up; Linda my partner was feeling fragile and needed to talk.
- I wanted to write my 3 pages and converse with my inner child.
- The house seemed in a tip and my son's gym kit needed sorting.

Sometimes life goes like this especially when our first thoughts when we wake up are beating ourselves up by thinking thoughts of fear in the future. So then I just put on a positive tape and started to listen with my unconscious mind, cooking the breakfast.

TIP 1. LEARN TO JUST STAND BACK AND LAUGH AT YOURSELF
Then I said out loud with my daughter laughing, "I am open and receptive to all good and the creativity of the universe now expresses through me". This changed my whole feeling inside and I started laughing at how funny I was, my attitude then just woke up and I began to say, "Whatever happens I will move towards my greatest good and I love life". We had a good breakfast and when alone I cleaned the fridge and hoovered the house. While cleaning I played with the dog and thought 'I am cleaning out the old beliefs in my mind'. The thought energy was now in the present and I stopped thinking about my meeting with the publisher tomorrow and what she might or might not say. She liked the book and encouraged me. Thank you infinite source.

TIP 2. LIVING NOW WITH YOUR SCARED INNER CHILD
Just notice that as soon as you are rehearsing the future negatively, your inner conversations between the inner child and inner parent can immediately leak your personal self worth, by choosing to think the worst. So make friends with your inner child. By asking in front of the mirror, "What would you like to do now, today?" My child said, "Go on the computer and write this up and lets have some fun creating". If I had stayed in my negative fear of the future, my old addiction of "Being rejected" would have come up to

make me feel a victim. Then I would have wanted rescuing and the old pattern would come up.

TIP 3. BE WILLING TO LEARN FROM EACH SITUATION

Every situation is our teacher nothing need be wasted. When we get stuck in old patterns just ask your higher self "What is going on and what do I need to learn?" Then the meaning and purpose will unfold and you will find yourself choosing positive affirmations. Like the one I am saying now is "All good will come from the meeting tomorrow and I send love to everyone I meet and contact today". This was not how I woke up! Now you maybe saying "Oh! I try to do that but I can't I haven't got time" and on and on. Well just be WILLING to change and grow in learning to love you a little each day. Remember "TRY" means you are unwilling, you won't or you'll set yourself up to fail, then you tell everybody you were right at knowing you were going to fail, this is such a waste of energy, stop and think thoughts that come from the higher self, the part of you that loves you. And so it is.

YOUR HEALING STORY

"Stories well told touch people: they resonate within people, because in the telling of something deeply human, that which is human is touched"
Ted Aoki Canadian educationalist.

"We all have a story, our healing story. Go beyond your fears to sharing the miracle you are."

"Divine love let the right publisher come with a loving intention that positively believes and supports the thoughts in this book. May this book help others to tell their healing story of loving the miracle they are! Each story published inspires others to learn love, joy, healing, and forgiveness and bring peace into our world. And so it is."

After writing this I then opened the writers and artists yearbook, and gave a rather weak outline to a publisher by email. My inner parent awoke this morning in panic, scolding my child for being so impulsive and thinking. "How dare you submit this book, this whole idea? You must be kidding yourself, you will get criticised unmercifully". Then after this negative self-talk between my inner parent and child, I stopped to see an old pattern of sabotaging my life. "Others can write you can't!" So I thanked that old belief and let it go with love.

I saw how I was holding my fear and setting up failure, the outcome of my first attempt was a polite rejection. My initial response was a mixture of hurt child and a scolding parent, saying, "I told you so." Then I went to the mirror and said, "I love you Roger keep learning and creating."

YOUR HEALING STORY

I am asking you to risk what you feel is appropriate; don't let fear hold you back. If fear does occur look at how you are holding that fear, what is the old thinking-feeling pattern that comes from your past. To write about your story is a step into a world that can seem risky, especially from the inner child's point of view. So if you have got this far into the book and are having an inner conversation with yourself, saying, "I can't write about me and how I have learnt to love me you must be kidding!" I understand you may have the thought, "What would other people say if they knew it was me?" You will make the right decision at the right time. Remember it will happen when your higher self prompts you.

Now remember the next book will be filled with stories that will make you cry, inspire you, laugh and begin a network of friendships across countries. You can be anonymous, or change your name.

If each of us is a miracle, even with our pain and hurt, we can communicate to each other our hopes, dreams, our overcoming? What has helped you grow and change positively and creatively? You may decide to write your own book, because as you write you find the universal mind encouraging you to develop your story into a book. Do read "The Artists Way" by Julia Cameron-just brilliant. What has helped you get through difficult relationships? How have you found the miracle inside you? We maybe ordinary, yet I believe we are extraordinary people, and truly magnificent when reconnected consciously to the intelligence that made us, we can heal this planet. I can hear you say "must be crazy, my story could only make things worse", well you could choose that thought!

A YEAR HAS PASSED

I have now started my own publishing company called Soul Talk Stories; this book is its first publication. As we go to press there are 30 submissions of different stories on our website, www.soultalkstories.com. As we build our miracle stories I hope people will read them aloud to friends and they will be stimulated to put pen to paper. One big lesson with little lessons on the way for me has been to use my "Magic" computer I believe writing your story and going beyond the hurt, will help you learn to love who you are, all the different parts of you. This will illuminate answers to the following: Who are you? What do you believe? About women, men, God, money, work, sex and any thinking feeling pattern that has conditioned you. You may think of people who have come into your life at critical times, who influenced you positively. Once you start, the story will take a life of meaning and direction. Keep affirming divine positive beliefs like.

"I am a channel for divine ideas to flow through me, everything I need will come to me at the right time and perfect space sequence. I now go beyond my limitations and other people's limitations."

I finish this book with a wonderful quote from Marianne Williamson. I encourage you to read her book "Return to love".

REMEMBER

"Our worst fear is not that we are inadequate; our deepest fear is that we are powerful beyond measure. It is our light not our darkness that most frightens us. We ask ourselves, 'Who am I to be brilliant, gorgeous, talented and fabulous!' Actually, who are you not to be? You are a child of God. Your playing small doesn't save the world. There is nothing enlightened about shrinking so that other people won't feel insecure around you. We are all meant to shine, as children do. We are born to make manifest the glory of God within us. It's not just in some of us; it's in everyone. And as we let our own light shine we unconsciously give other people permission to do the same. As we're liberated from our own fear, our presence automatically liberates others."

This quote is often incorrectly attributed to Nelson Mandela and his inaugural speech. Perhaps this wonderful mistake is saying "no physical prison can hold back the unfolding miracle in each of us when we each make a deep commitment to loving the miracle we truly are". When you make a deep commitment to free and release your mind and body from the past and learn to love and live your unfolding miracle, no prison can hold you and then we can contribute to healing our planet now and in the future for all the children to come and play in this school of life.

GUIDELINES TO UNFOLDING YOUR MIRACLE STORY

As I have meditated about the idea of publishing your stories, I have asked the universal power to find the best way to do this, so love, peace and healing are sent around the earth. As I write this I have the thought of setting up a website where we could publish your stories, this is now done.

Two creative men Vidya and John have built a website where you can download this book and 'The Little Book of Thoughts' plus beautiful posters of loving our 'inner child' affirmations at www.soultalkstories.com.

SUGGESTED FRAMEWORK

1. I would like you to keep the story to 2000 words. I know this maybe difficult, have fun doing it. Please see the stories already online and the categories on the website. They range from fun, death, spirit, "How I met my soul mate?" and many more. By following simple procedures you can submit each story or poem yourself.

2. Meditate on the following questions.

• What is your story?

• What has helped you to heal and prosper in your life? Your unique process.
• What is your new picture of yourself? What have you come to learn and teach?

• What has changed?

Thank you for taking your time to read this book. Do read the stories on www.soultalkstories.com; I salute each person who took the risk to shine there light I hope they spark the power within you and encourage you to love you.

Please contact me on roger@soultalkstories.com.

I send love to you all.

Roger.

RECOMMENDED READING

'Anatomy of the Spirit', by Caroline Myss, Ph.D.

The following by Dr Wayne Dyer 'Manifest Your Destiny', 'Wisdom of The Ages' 'What Do You Really Want for Your Children' and 'Your Erroneous Zones'.

Any of the following by Louise L. Hay 'You can Heal Your Life'.
'You Can Heal Your Life Companion Book', 'Empowering Women'.
'The Power is Within You', 'A Garden of Thoughts: My Affirmation Journal'.
'Heal Your Body', Any of Louise Hays Self Help Tapes. Visit www.hayhouse.com

'End The Struggle and Dance with Life', and 'Feel The Fear and Do It Anyway', by Susan Jeffers Ph.D.

'Minding the body, Mending the Mind', by Joan Borysenko
Visit www.joanborysenko.com

'Creating Money Keys to Abundance' by Sanaya Roman & Duane Packer.

'Be Your Own Life Coach', by Fiona Harrold.

'A Return to Love', by Marianne Williamson

'A Course In Miracles, Foundation For Inner Peace', ISBN 0-9606388-2-2.

'Self-Parenting', by John K Pollard III. Visit www.selfparenting.com

'Homecoming', by John Bradshaw.

'Love Medicine & Miracles', and 'Living, Loving & Healing' by Bernie Segal, M.D.

'Sixty Minute Father', by Rob Parsons.

'Courage To Heal', by Ellen Bass & Laura Davis.

'Recovering from abuse. The Trauma Trap' by Dr David Muss, 'self help book for People suffering Post-Traumatic Stress Disorder

Trauma & Recovery', by Dr Judith Herman

Carl Rogers on Personal Power, 'Three Marriages and one growing person' by Carl Rogers

'The Creative Connection', 'The Emerging Woman', both by Natalie Rogers.

'The Artist's Way', 'The Right to Write', both by Julia Cameron

'Practical Miracles for Mars and Venus', by John Gray.

'The Science of Mind', by Earnest Holmes.

'Soul Searching (a Girl's Guide to Finding Herself)', by Sarah Stillman.

Any of the Following by Catherine Ponder

'The Healing Secrets of the Ages'. 'The Dynamic Laws of Healing'.
'The Dynamic Laws Of Prosperity'.

'Better Relationships' by Sarah Litvinoff.

'More Positive Thinking' by Vera Peiffer.

'Positive News' visit www.positivenews.net

'Boundless Love', by Miranda Holden.

'Women Who Love Too Much', by Robin Norwood.

'Self Esteem', by Gael Lindenfield.(has written many good books)

'The Alchemist' by Paulo Coelho.

'Opening Doors Within', by Eileen Caddy.

Plus many good books from Findhorn. Visit www.findhornpress.com

'What is the New Age still saying to The Church' by John Drane.

'Chicken Soup for the Soul', & 'Chicken Soup for the Teenage Soul', both by Jack Canfield & Mark Victor Hanson

'Food combining For Health' by Doris Grant & Jean Joyce.

'The Prophet', by Kahlil Gibran.

Websites that are inspiring and are Creating a circle of love on this planet.

www.inspirationline.com, Chelle Thompson sends a twice-weekly newsletter free.

www.possibilitiesinaction.com. Karin Peterson-Sitrin a personal coach.

www.vidyawebwisesage.com. Vidya who builds websites like www.soultalkstories.com

'Love The Miracle you Are'
©Roger King & John Welding 2003

Written by Roger King
roger@soultalkstories.com

Illustrations and Design by John Welding
mailto:john.welding@ukonline.co.uk
Visit the website at www.soultalkstories.com